Nginx Module Extension

Customize and regulate the robust Nginx web server,
and write your own Nginx modules efficiently

Usama Dar

BIRMINGHAM - MUMBAI

Nginx Module Extension

First published: December 2013

Production Reference: 1191213

Published by Packt Publishing Ltd.
Livery Place
35 Livery Street
Birmingham B3 2PB, UK.

ISBN 978-1-78216-304-6

www.packtpub.com

Cover Image by Rakesh Shejwal (shejwal.rakesh@gmail.com)

Credits

Author
Usama Dar

Reviewer
Alex Kapranoff

Acquisition Editor
Rebecca Youe

Commissioning Editor
Manasi Pandire

Technical Editors
Aparna Chand
Aparna Kumari
Adrian Raposo

Copy Editors
Janbal Dharmaraj
Dipti Kapadia
Karuna Narayanan
Alfida Paiva

Project Coordinator
Amey Sawant

Proofreader
Ting Baker

Indexer
Rekha Nair

Production Coordinator
Melwyn D'sa

Cover Work
Melwyn D'sa

About the Author

Usama Dar has over 13 years' experience working with software systems. During this period, he has not only worked with large companies such as Nortel Networks, Ericsson, and Huawei, but has also been involved with successful startups such as EnterpriseDB. He has worked with systems with mission-critical requirements of scalability and high availability. He writes actively on this website: www.usamadar.com. These days, Usama works at the Huawei Research Centre in Munich, where he spends most of his time researching highly scalable, high-performing infrastructure software (such as operating systems), databases, and web and application servers.

Big thanks to my parents for always providing me with confidence to pursue my dreams. Thanks to my wife for putting up with my crazy schedule and allowing me to work at odd hours to complete this book.

About the Reviewer

Alex Kapranoff was born into the family of an electronics engineer and programmer for the old Soviet "Big Iron" computers. He started programming at the age of 12 and has never worked outside the IT industry since. After earning a degree in Software Engineering with honors, he had a short stint in the world of enterprise databases and Windows. Then he settled on open source, Unix-like environments for good, first FreeBSD and then Linux, working as a developer for many Russian companies from ISPs to search engines. Most of his experience has been with e-mail and messaging systems and web security. Right now, he is trying his hand at a product and project management position in Yandex, one of the biggest search engines in the world.

He took his first look at Nginx working in Rambler side by side with the author of Nginx, Igor Sysoev, before the initial public release of the product. Since then, Nginx has been an essential tool in his kit. He doesn't launch a website—no matter how complex it is—without using Nginx.

He strongly believes in the Free Software Movement, loves Perl, plain C, LISP, cooking, and fishing, and lives with a beautiful girlfriend and an old cat in Moscow, Russia.

www.PacktPub.com

Support files, eBooks, discount offers and more

You might want to visit www.PacktPub.com for support files and downloads related to your book.

Did you know that Packt offers eBook versions of every book published, with PDF and ePub files available? You can upgrade to the eBook version at www.PacktPub.com and as a print book customer, you are entitled to a discount on the eBook copy. Get in touch with us at service@packtpub.com for more details.

At www.PacktPub.com, you can also read a collection of free technical articles, sign up for a range of free newsletters and receive exclusive discounts and offers on Packt books and eBooks.

http://PacktLib.PacktPub.com

Do you need instant solutions to your IT questions? PacktLib is Packt's online digital book library. Here, you can access, read and search across Packt's entire library of books.

Why Subscribe?
- Fully searchable across every book published by Packt
- Copy and paste, print and bookmark content
- On demand and accessible via web browser

Free Access for Packt account holders

If you have an account with Packt at www.PacktPub.com, you can use this to access PacktLib today and view nine entirely free books. Simply use your login credentials for immediate access.

Table of Contents

Preface

This book is for advanced users such as system administrators and developers who want to extend Nginx's functionality using its highly flexible add-on system. We look at the existing modules available and how to compile and install them, along with practical examples of how to configure them with focus on optimizing the configuration. It also goes beyond what is available off the shelf and teaches you how to write your own module, in case something is not available from the big Nginx open source community.

What this book covers

Chapter 1, *Installing Nginx Core and Modules from Source*, serves as a quick reference for downloading and installing Nginx and compilation options related to different modules and add-ons.

Chapter 2, *Configuring Core Modules*, is a reference to the core modules in Nginx, which cannot be disabled, and explores different configuration options for them.

Chapter 3, *Installing and Configuring HTTP Modules*, is a reference to the standard and optional HTTP modules, their synopsis, directives as well as practical configuration examples.

Chapter 4, *Installing Third-party Modules*, introduces third-party modules, mostly available on GitHub. It talks about some well-known third-party modules, their installation and configuration, and also some guidelines on how to find different third-party modules out there.

Chapter 5, *Creating Your Own Module*, gives a brief introduction to creating your own modules. This chapter is a quick reference to the module system in Nginx. It also has a quick reference to the internal architecture of Nginx, which makes extension possible.

What you need for this book

This book will help you understand the module-based architecture of Nginx. You will learn to install Nginx as well as extend it with several available modules. This book specially touches on the topic of creating your own Nginx modules. Most people have to read heaps of code to get this done. This book will make it easier for advanced users who are looking to extend Nginx by not only using existing modules, but also writing something of their own.

Who this book is for

This book is intended for advanced users, system administrators, and developers of Nginx modules.

Conventions

In this book, you will find a number of styles of text that distinguish between different kinds of information. Here are some examples of these styles, and an explanation of their meaning.

Code words in text, database table names, folder names, filenames, file extensions, pathnames, dummy URLs, user input, and Twitter handles are shown as follows: "You can reload the Nginx configuration once you edit the `nginx.conf` file."

A block of code is set as follows:

```
[nginx]
name=nginx repo
baseurl=http://nginx.org/packages/centos/$releasever/
    $basearch/
gpgcheck=0
enabled=1
```

When we wish to draw your attention to a particular part of a code block, the relevant lines or items are set in bold:

```
ngx_uint_t          spare0;
ngx_uint_t          spare1;
ngx_uint_t          spare2;
ngx_uint_t          spare3;
ngx_uint_t          version;
void                *ctx;
```

Any command-line input or output is written as follows:

```
# cd /usr/ports/www/nginx
# make install clean
```

New terms and **important words** are shown in bold. Words that you see on the screen, in menus or dialog boxes, for example, appear in the text like this: "For example, according to the following configuration, this module will make sure that it prints **Hello World**."

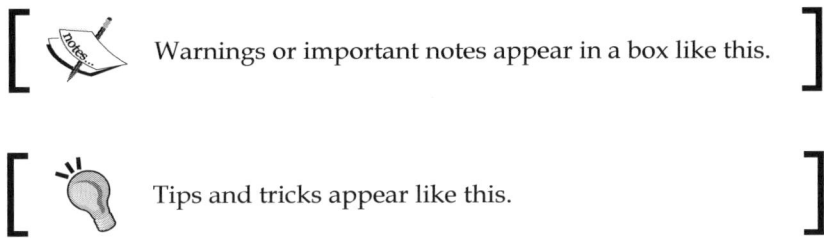

Warnings or important notes appear in a box like this.

Tips and tricks appear like this.

Reader feedback

Feedback from our readers is always welcome. Let us know what you think about this book—what you liked or may have disliked. Reader feedback is important for us to develop titles that you really get the most out of.

To send us general feedback, simply send an e-mail to feedback@packtpub.com, and mention the book title via the subject of your message.

If there is a topic that you have expertise in and you are interested in either writing or contributing to a book, see our author guide on www.packtpub.com/authors.

Customer support

Now that you are the proud owner of a Packt book, we have a number of things to help you to get the most from your purchase.

Errata

Although we have taken every care to ensure the accuracy of our content, mistakes do happen. If you find a mistake in one of our books—maybe a mistake in the text or the code—we would be grateful if you would report this to us. By doing so, you can save other readers from frustration and help us improve subsequent versions of this book. If you find any errata, please report them by visiting http://www.packtpub.com/submit-errata, selecting your book, clicking on the **errata submission form** link, and entering the details of your errata. Once your errata are verified, your submission will be accepted and the errata will be uploaded on our website, or added to any list of existing errata, under the Errata section of that title. Any existing errata can be viewed by selecting your title from http://www.packtpub.com/support.

Piracy

Piracy of copyright material on the Internet is an ongoing problem across all media. At Packt, we take the protection of our copyright and licenses very seriously. If you come across any illegal copies of our works, in any form, on the Internet, please provide us with the location address or website name immediately so that we can pursue a remedy.

Please contact us at copyright@packtpub.com with a link to the suspected pirated material.

We appreciate your help in protecting our authors, and our ability to bring you valuable content.

Questions

You can contact us at questions@packtpub.com if you are having a problem with any aspect of the book, and we will do our best to address it.

1
Installing Nginx Core and Modules from Source

This chapter serves as a quick reference to downloading and installing Nginx using binary and source distribution and compilation options related to different modules and add-ons.

If you are reading this book, you are already familiar with Nginx (pronounced as engine-x). Therefore, we will not spend too much time discussing the basics. However, you will need a working copy of Nginx before proceeding to advanced topics.

Installing binary distribution

Most UNIX and Linux distributions have Nginx included in their package manager repositories. Use package manager commands on your platform to install it. For example, use **apt-get** on Ubuntu or Debian, and **emerge** on Gentoo. For Red Hat, Fedora, or CentOS, see the instructions that follow.

You can find binary installation instructions for different platforms such as Red Hat and Ubuntu on the Nginx installation wiki at `http://wiki.nginx.org/Install`. However, we will briefly describe the process here, quoting from the wiki.

Red Hat, Fedora, and CentOS

To add the Nginx yum repository, create a file named `/etc/yum.repos.d/nginx.repo` and paste one of the following configurations:

- **For CentOS**:

  ```
  [nginx]
  name=nginx repo
  baseurl=http://nginx.org/packages/centos/$releasever/
    $basearch/
  gpgcheck=0
  enabled=1
  ```

- **For RHEL**:

  ```
  [nginx]
  name=nginx repo
  baseurl=http://nginx.org/packages/rhel/$releasever/
    $basearch/
  gpgcheck=0
  enabled=1
  ```

CentOS, RHEL, and Scientific Linux, each populate the `$releasever` variable differently. Therefore, depending on your OS version, replace `$releasever` with 5 (for 5.x) or 6 (for 6.x). Therefore, `baseurl` for 6.x would look like `baseurl=http://nginx.org/packages/rhel/6/$basearch/`.

Official Debian/Ubuntu packages

Append the following lines to the `/etc/apt/sources.list` file, and replace the codename with the one appropriate for the release that you are using, for example, Ubuntu 13.10 is codenamed `saucy`:

- **For Ubuntu 12.10**:

  ```
  deb http://nginx.org/packages/ubuntu/ saucy nginx
  deb-src http://nginx.org/packages/ubuntu/ saucy nginx
  ```

  Please note that when you will run the apt-get update after adding the repository, you will get a **GPG** error of not being able to verify keys. If this happens and you find it hard to ignore it, do the following:

  ```
  wget http://nginx.org/packages/keys/nginx_signing.key
  cat nginx_signing.key | sudo apt-key add -
  ```

- **For Debian 6**:

  ```
  deb http://nginx.org/packages/debian/ squeeze nginx
  deb-src http://nginx.org/packages/debian/ squeeze nginx
  ```

- **For Ubuntu PPA**: This PPA is maintained by volunteers and is not distributed by nginx.org. It has some additional compiled-in modules, and it may be more fitting for your environment. You can get the latest stable version of Nginx from **Nginx PPA** on Launchpad: You will require root privileges to execute the following commands.

  ○ **For Ubuntu 10.04 and newer**:

    ```
    sudo -s

    nginx=stable # use nginx=development for latest
    development version

    add-apt-repository ppa:nginx/$nginx

    apt-get update

    apt-get install nginx
    ```

If you get an error about add-apt-repository not existing, you will want to install python-software-properties. For other Debian/Ubuntu based distributions, you can try the lucid variant of the PPA that is the most likely to work on older package sets.

```
sudo -s

nginx=stable # use nginx=development for latest development
  version

echo "deb http://ppa.launchpad.net/nginx/$nginx/ubuntu lucid
  main" > /etc/apt/sources.list.d/nginx-$nginx-lucid.list

apt-key adv --keyserver keyserver.ubuntu.com --recv-keys
  C300EE8C

apt-get update

apt-get install nginx
```

FreeBSD

Update the BSD ports tree using the following command:

```
# portsnap fetch update
```

Install the web server using the following commands:

```
# cd /usr/ports/www/nginx
# make install clean
```

Type the following command to turn the Nginx server on:

```
echo 'nginx_enable="YES"' >> /etc/rc.conf
```

To start Nginx, enter:

```
# /usr/local/etc/rc.d/nginx start
```

OpenBSD

OpenBSD, as of Version 5.1, includes Nginx as part of the base system. This means Nginx comes pre-installed along with all the library dependencies. The version is not always the latest and greatest one. However, this allows you to start migrating Apache applications over to Nginx. In the future, it is expected that the default httpd will be Nginx instead of Apache.

Official Win32 binaries

As of Version 0.8.50 of Nginx, the official Windows binary is now available.

The Windows version is provided as binary-only due to the current build process, which uses WineTools at the moment. You will not be able to compile a Windows version from source. Once you download the Windows ZIP file, perform the following steps:

1. **Installation**:

   ```
   cd c:\
   unzip nginx-1.2.3.zip
   ren nginx-1.2.3 nginx
   cd nginx
   start nginx
   ```

2. **Control**:

   ```
   nginx -s [ stop | quit | reopen | reload ]
   ```

For problems, look in the `c:\nginx\logs\error.log` file or in `EventLog`.

Installing source distribution

Nginx binary packages are outdated and usually have an older version. If the binaries on your platform are not the latest and up-to-date, you can download the source from `http://nginx.org/en/download.html`. At the time of writing this chapter, Version 1.4.3 is the stable downloadable version.

You can also checkout or clone the latest source.

Read-only Subversion repositories:

`code: svn://svn.nginx.org/nginx`

Read-only Mercurial repositories:

`site: http://hg.nginx.org/nginx.org`

After you have downloaded the source archive, un-tar it and use the following standard build commands to build a standard binary:

```
./configure
make
sudo make install
```

This places the Nginx binary under `user/local`. However, you can override this path through configure options.

Nginx library dependencies

If you want to build Nginx from source, the following libraries are needed at the minimum:

- GCC
- Autotools (automake and autoconf)
- PCRE (Perl Compatible Regular Expressions)
- zlib
- OpenSSL

You also have the option to disable the dependency on PCRE, zlib, and OpenSSL by disabling the compilation of rewrite, gzip, and ssl modules. These modules are enabled by default.

Configuring options

Compile-time options are provided through `configure`. You can also find documentation related to the configure-time options online at `http://wiki.nginx.org/InstallOptions`.

The `configure` command defines various aspects of the system including the methods that Nginx is allowed to use for connection processing. At the end, it creates a makefile. You can use `./configure --help` to see a full list of options supported by the `configure` command.

The following section is extracted from the Nginx online wiki.

Files and permissions

- `--prefix=path`: It is set to the `/usr/local/nginx` directory by default. The path specified here is the root folder for keeping the server files. This includes the executable files, server log files, configuration files, and html documentation.

- `--sbin-path=path`: The default Nginx executable name is `/sbin/nginx`. You can change the name using this configure option.

- `--conf-path=path`: The default for this option is `prefix/conf/nginx.conf`. This is the default path for the Nginx configuration file. This file, as you will learn later, is used to configure everything about the Nginx server. The path also contains a number of other configuration files such as a sample `fastcgi` configuration file and character-set maps. You can always change this path later on in the configuration file.

- `--pid-path=path`: This option allows you to change the name of the pid file. The pid files are used by various utilities (including start/stop scripts) to determine if the server is running. Normally, it is a plain text file with the server process ID in it. By default, the file is named `prefix/logs/nginx.pid`.

- `--error-log-path=path`: This option allows you to specify the location of the error log. By default, the file is named `prefix/logs/error.log`. You can set this value to `stderr`. It will redirect all the error messages to the standard error on your system. Normally, this will be your console or the screen.

- `--http-log-path=path`: This sets the name of the log file where all HTTP requests are logged. By default, the file is named `prefix/logs/access.log`. Like other options, this can be changed anytime by providing the `access_log` directive in the configuration file.

- `--user=USER`: This sets the username that will be used to run the Nginx worker processes. You should make sure that this is an unprivileged or non-root user. The default user name is `nobody`. You can change it later through the `user` directive in the configuration file.

- `--group=name`: This sets the name of the group used to run the worker processes. The default group name is `nobody`. You can change this through the `user` directive in the configuration file.

The Event loop

One of the reasons for Nginx being so fast and stable is its ability to use event-based functions. Input/Output. The event-based coding ensures maximum performance within a single core by allowing it to be non-blocking. However, event-based code needs the underlying platform support such as kqueue (FreeBSD, NetBSD, OpenBSD, and OSX), epoll (Linux), and /dev/poll (Solaris, HPUX).In cases where these methods are not available, Nginx can work with more traditional select() and poll() methods as well. The following options affect this behavior:

* --with-select_module
* --without-select_module

These enable or disable building of a module that allows the server to work with the select() method. This module is built automatically if the platform does not appear to support more appropriate methods such as kqueue, epoll, rtsig, or /dev/poll.

* --with-poll_module
* --without-poll_module

These enable or disable the building of a module that allows the server to work with the poll() method. This module is built automatically if the platform does not appear to support more appropriate methods such as kqueue, epoll, rtsig, or /dev/poll.

Optional modules

The optional modules are as follows:

* --without-http_gzip_module: This option allows you to disable over-the-wire compression. This can be quite useful if you are sending or receiving large text documents over HTTP. However, if you don't want to build this compression into Nginx binary, or you don't have access to the zlib library that is required to enable this support, you can disable it using this option.

* --without-http_rewrite_module: This option allows you to disable the HTTP rewrite module. The HTTP rewrite module allows you to redirect HTTP requests by modifying URIs that match a given pattern. You need the PCRE library to enable this module.

* --without-http_proxy_module: This disables ngx_http_proxy_module. The proxy module allows you to pass the HTTP request to another server.

* --with-http_ssl_module: This enables the SSL support in the server. This is not enabled by default and you need OpenSSL in order to build SSL support in the Nginx binary.

- `--with-pcre=path`: If you have downloaded the PCRE source on your machine, you can provide its path through this parameter. Nginx will automatically build this library before building the Nginx server. Please make sure that the version of PCRE source is 4.4 or higher.

- `--with-pcre-jit`: This builds the PCRE library with the "just-in-time compilation" support. This is significantly to improve the pattern matching or rewriting speed by converting the regular expressions into machine code.

- `--with-zlib=path`: If you have already downloaded the zlib library source, you can provide its path here. Nginx will build the zlib library before building the server binary. Please make sure that the source version is 1.1.3 or higher.

Compilation controls

The compilation controls are as follows:

- `--with-cc-opt=parameters`: Additional options for the CFLAGS variable

- `--with-ld-opt=parameters`: Additional parameters for the linker (`LD_LIBRARY_PATH`) that you should provide `--with-ld-opt="-L /usr/local/lib` when building on FreeBSD

Example

Example of parameters usage (all of this needs to be typed in one line):

```
./configure
    --sbin-path=/usr/local/nginx/nginx
    --conf-path=/usr/local/nginx/nginx.conf
    --pid-path=/usr/local/nginx/nginx.pid
    --with-http_ssl_module
    --with-pcre=../pcre-4.4
    --with-zlib=../zlib-1.1.3
```

> When using the system PCRE library under FreeBSD, the following options should be specified:
> - --with-ld-opt="-L /usr/local/lib" \
> - --with-cc-opt="-I /usr/local/include"
>
> If the number of files supported by `select()` needs to be increased, it can also be specified like this:
> - --with-cc-opt="-D FD_SETSIZE=2048"

The Custom module

One of the great strengths of Nginx is its modular design. You are able to hook in third-party modules or modules that you write yourself.

`--add-module=path` compiles the module located at `path` into Nginx binary. You can find a list of third-party modules available for Nginx at `http://wiki.nginx.org/3rdPartyModules`.

Debugging

`--with-debug` enables debug logging. This option is already enabled in the Windows binary. Once you compile Nginx with this option, you then have to set the debug level with the `error_log` directive in the configuration file, and so on:

```
error_log /path/to/log debug
```

In addition to debug logging, you can also attach a debugger to a running version of Nginx. If you intend to do so, enable the debugging symbols in the Nginx binary. Compile with `-g` or `-ggdb` and recommended compiler optimization level of `O0` or `O2` (this makes the debugger output easier to understand). The optimization level `O3` auto-vectorizes the code and introduces certain other optimizations that make debugging harder. Set the CFLAGS environment variable as follows and run `configure`:

```
CFLAGS="-g -O0" ./configure ...
```

Installing on other platforms

Let us install Nginx on other platforms such as the following:

- Gentoo: To get the latest version of Nginx, add a platform mask in your portage configuration file `/etc/portage/package.keywords`

  `www-servers/nginx ~x86 (or ~amd64, etc)`

- X86/ 64 builds for Solaris are available on `http://joyent.com/blog/ok-nginx-is-cool`

- MacOSX: Install Xcode or Xcode command-line tools to get all the required compilers and libraries

- A detailed account of how to resolve dependencies like PCRE and others is described in detail for Solaris 10 u5 `http://wiki.nginx.org/Installing_on_Solaris_10_u5`

Verifying your Nginx installation

Following are the steps to verify that Nginx has been installed:

1. Once you have successfully compiled and built Nginx, verify it by running the `nginx -V` command.

2. As a root user, run the Nginx server using `prefix/ nginx/sbin/nginx`.

3. You will see the `nginx.pid` file once the server is running. The location of this file depends on the option that you provided while running the configure script. On Ubuntu, the default location is `/var/run/nginx.pid`.

You can reload the Nginx configuration once you edit the `nginx.conf` file. To do this, send SIGNUP to the main process. The PID of this process is in the `nginx.pid` file. The following command will reload the configuration on Ubuntu:

```
kill -HUP `cat var/run/nginx.pid
```

Summary

In this chapter, we learned how to download binary and source releases of Nginx and install binary releases. We have also learned how to compile and install Nginx from source, how to override installation paths and other properties using configure options, how to compile Nginx with debugging symbols, and finally, how to verify the installation.

In the next chapter, we will learn more about configuration of core Nginx modules.

Configuring Core Modules

2

In this chapter we will explore the configuration of the `Main` and `Events` modules of Nginx, which are also called the core modules. We will discuss the module-related configuration options and important points that one needs to remember while using these options.

Understanding the Main module

The Nginx `Main` module consists of the following configuration directives or commands:

Name	Value	Default	Example
daemon	on, off	on	
master_process	on, off	on	
timer_resolution	interval	0	100ms
pid	file	logs/nginx.pid	/var/log/nginx.pid
lock_file	file	logs/nginx.lock	/var/log/nginx.lock
worker_processes	number, auto	1	2
debug_points	stop, abort	null	stop
user	user [group]	nobody nobody	www users
worker_priority	number	0	15
worker_cpu_affinity	cpu mask		0101 1010
worker_rlimit_nofile	number		1000
worker_rlimit_core	size		500M
worker_rlimit_sigpending	number		1000
working_directory	directory	compile time	/usr/local/nginx
env	variable = value		PERL5LIB=/data/site/modules

Explaining directives

We will now discuss all the `Main` module's directives mentioned in the preceding table in detail.

daemon

The `daemon` directive determines if Nginx will run in the daemon mode. A daemon (or a service) is a background process that is designed to run autonomously, with little or no user intervention. Since Version 1.0.9 of Nginx, it is safe to run Nginx with this option turned off. It is not possible to do a binary upgrade of Nginx without stopping it, if this option is off.

Nginx's master process is responsible for nonstop binary upgrades. The signal that is used for this purpose is `SIGUSR2`. However, when the daemon mode is off, this signal is ignored because the master process will still have the old binary. This is unlike the daemon mode, where the parent of the new worker process is switched to the `Init` process, and therefore, you can start a new worker process with new binaries. The only reason you might want to run the daemon mode with `master_process` off would be for debugging purposes. Turning these options off will run Nginx in the foreground without a master process, and you can terminate it simply by pressing *Ctrl* + *R*. However, you should not run Nginx in production without the daemon mode and `master_process`.

master_process

The `master_process` directive determines if Nginx will run with a master process. It has many responsibilities in Nginx, including spawning off worker processes. Nginx will run in the single-process mode if you set `master_process` off. You should always run in production with the `master_process` option turned on. The only reason you might want to turn `master_process` off is for debugging reasons, as it might be much simpler to debug the code in a single-process mode.

timer_resolution

Setting the `timer_resolution` directive will reduce the number of `gettimeofday()` system calls. Instead of doing this system call for each kernel event, `gettimeofday()` is only called once per specified interval. You might want to turn this option off if `gettimeofday()` shows up as an overhead on a busy server. You won't notice any difference on an idle server though. One good reason to use `timer_resolution` is to get the exact time in logs for the upstream response times.

pid

The `pid` directive specifies the filename for the `PID` file of the master process. The default value is relative to the `--prefix` configure option.

lock_file

The `lock_file` directive specifies the filename of the lock file. The default value is relative to the `--prefix` configure option. You can also specify this option during the compile time through the following configure script:

```
./configure --lock-path=/var/log/nginx.lock
```

worker_processes

The `worker_processes` directive defines the maximum number of worker processes. A worker process is a single-threaded process spawned by the master process. If you set this option to `auto`, Nginx will automatically try to determine the number of CPUs/core and set this option equal to that number. The `auto` parameter is supported starting from Versions 1.3.8 and 1.2.5. If you want Nginx to only use a limited number of cores on your server, setting this value explicitly would be a good idea.

debug_points

The `debug_points` directive is useful to debug Nginx. If you set this directive to `abort`, Nginx will produce a core dump file whenever there is an internal error. You can use this core dump file to obtain an error trace in a system debugger such as `gdb`. In order to obtain the core dump file, you will also need to configure the `working_rlimit_core` and `working_directory` directives.

If this directive is set to `stop`, any internal error will lead to the stopping of the process.

user

The `user` directive is used to specify the user and the group of the worker processes. If no group name is specified, the same group name as that of the user is used. You can override the default nobody nobody by specifying the user and the group with the following `configure` script:

```
./configure --user=www --group=users
```

worker_priority

The `worker_priority` directive allows you to set the nice priority of the worker processes. Nginx will use the `setpriority()` system call to set the priority. Setting the priority to a lower value can result in favorable scheduling of the worker processes.

The actual priority range varies between kernel versions. Before 1.3.36, Linux had a range from –infinity to 15. Since kernel 1.3.43, Linux has the range from -20 to 19. On some systems, the range of nice values is from -20 to 20.

worker_cpu_affinity

The `worker_cpu_affinity` directive allows you to set the affinity masks for the worker processes. Affinity masks are bit masks, which can bind a process to a certain CPU. This can lead to better performance on some systems such as Windows, where several system processes are restricted to the first CPU/core. Therefore, excluding the first CPU/core can lead to better performance. We can bind each worker process to a different CPU with the following code snippet:

```
worker_processes     4;
worker_cpu_affinity 0001 0010 0100 1000;
```

You can set the CPU affinity value to up to 64 CPU/core.

worker_rlimit_nofile

The `worker_rlimit_nofile` directive sets the maximum limit on open files (`RLIMIT_NOFILE`) that a worker process can use. When this directive is set, the `setrlimit()` system call is used to set the resource limit. Any attempt to exceed this limit will result in an error `EFILE` (signifying too many open files).

worker_rlimit_core

The `worker_rlimit_core` directive sets the maximum size of the core dump file created by a worker process. When this option is set, the `setrlimit()` system call is used to set the resource limit of the file size. When this option is `0`, no core dump files are created.

worker_rlimit_sigpending

The `worker_rlimit_sigpending` directive specifies the limit on the number of signals that may be queued for the real user ID of the calling process. If you are using a Linux kernel version newer than 2.6.6, it will support real-time signals (`rtsig`), and each process will have its own queue as opposed to a system-wide queue in the earlier implementations. When this option is set, a `setrlimit()` system call is used to set the resource limit `RLIMIT_SIGPENDING`. In order to enforce this limit, both standard and real-time signals are counted.

working_directory

The `working_directory` directive specifies the path where the core dump files are created. This path should be an absolute path. You must make sure that the user or group specified via the `user` option has a write permission in this folder.

env

The `env` directive allows you to set some environment variables, which will be inherited by the worker processes. If you set some environment variables on a shell, they will be erased by Nginx, except `TZ`. This directive allows you to preserve some of the inherited variables, change their values, or create new environment variables. The environment variable `NGINX` is used internally by the server and should not be set by the user.

If you specify an environment variable's name without specifying its value, the value from the parent process, that is, the shell will be retained by Nginx. But if you specify a value as well, this new value will be used by the server.

```
env MALLOC_OPTIONS;
env PERL5LIB=/data/site/modules;
env OPENSSL_ALLOW_PROXY_CERTS=1;
```

In the preceding code snippet, the value of the environment variable `MALLOC_OPTIONS` is retained from the parent process, while the other two environment variables are defined or redefined and any value set by the parent process is wiped off.

Understanding the Events module

The `Events` module deals with the configuration of `epoll`, `kqueue`, `select`, `poll`, and more. This module consists of the following directives:

Name	Value	Default	Example
accept_mutex	on, off	on	off
accept_mutex_delay	interval (ms)	500ms	500ms
debug_connection	ip, cidr	none	192.168.1.1
devpoll_changes	number	32	64
devpoll_events	number	32	64
kqueue_changes	number	512	512

Name	Value	Default	Example
kqueue_events	number	512	512
epoll_events	number	512	512
multi_accept	on, off	off	on
rtsig_signo	signal number	SIGRTMIN+10	
rtsig_overflow_events	number	16	24
rtsig_overflow_test	number	32	40
rtsig_overflow_threshold	number	10	3
use	Kqueue, rtsig, epoll, /dev/poll, select	decided by the configure script	rtsig
worker_connections	number	512	200

Explaining directives

We will now discuss the Events module's directives summarized in the preceding table, in detail.

accept_mutex

The accept_mutex directive tries to prevent workers from competing over accept() for listing sockets (in the kernel). In other words, without accept_mutex, workers may try to simultaneously check for new events on sockets, which may lead to a slight increase in the CPU usage. Depending on your OS and the event-notification mechanisms, the results may vary. If you are using rtsig as the signal-processing mechanism, this option needs to be enabled.

accept_mutex_delay

As enabling accept_mutex serializes the accept() call from worker processes, that is, one worker process does one accept at a time, the accept_mutex_delay directive determines how long the other worker processes will wait before they are ready to accept new connections while another process is already doing it.

debug_connection

In order to use the debug_connection directive, Nginx needs to be built with the --debug-enabled option while running the configure script. You can specify the IPv4 or IPv6 address of the clients for which the debugging log will be enabled. You can also provide a domain name or unix: for Unix domain socket connections. The log level for the rest of the clients is determined through the error_log option. The debug log is written to the logfile specified in the `error_log` option as defined in the following code snippet:

```
error_log /var/log/nginx-error.log;
events {
    debug_connection 127.0.0.1;
    debug_connection localhost;
    debug_connection 192.0.2.0/24;
    debug_connection ::1;
    debug_connection 2001:0db8::/32;
    debug_connection unix:;
    ...
}
```

devpoll_changes and devpoll_events

The `/dev/poll` directive is an efficient method used in Solaris 7 11/99+, HP/UX 11.22+ (eventport), IRIX 6.5.15+, and Tru64 UNIX 5.1A+. The `devpoll_changes` and `devpoll_events` parameters define the number of changes and events that can move to and from the kernel. Nginx only writes the `devpoll_changes` or `devpoll_events` number of events and changes to `/dev/poll` at a time while processing events.

kqueue_changes and kqueue_events

The `kqueue` directive is an efficient event-notification interface used in FreeBSD 4.1+, OpenBSD 2.9+, NetBSD 2.0, and Mac OS X. It provides efficient input and output event pipelines between the `kernel` and `user` processes. It is possible to receive pending events while using only a single system call `kevent()`. This contrasts with older traditional polling system calls such as `poll` and `select`, which are less efficient, especially while polling for events on a large number of file descriptors. Other advanced event mechanisms such as `/dev/poll` and `epoll` allow you to do the same.

These parameters control how many changes and events are passed at a time to the `kevent()` system call.

epoll_events

The `epoll_events` directive is an efficient event-notification method used in Linux 2.6+. There are patches present to port this functionality to older kernels as well. This parameter determines the buffer size where the events are returned at a time before they are processed.

multi_accept

The worker process will try to accept all or as many incoming connections as possible when the multi_accept directive is enabled. Turning this option off will result in worker processes only accepting one connection at a time. This option is ignored if the kqueue_events notification method is used. If you use the rtsig method, this option is automatically enabled. By default, this option is turned off. It can be a high-performance tweak; however, the bad thing with multi_accept is that if you have a constant stream of incoming connections at a high rate, it may overflow your worker_connections directive without any chance of processing the already-accepted connections.

rtsig_signo

Linux supports 32 real-time signals, numbered from 32 (SIGRTMIN) to 63 (SIGRTMAX). Programs should always refer to real-time signals using the notation SIGRTMIN+n, since the range of real-time signal numbers varies across *nix platforms. Nginx uses two signals when the rtsig method is used. The directive specifies the first signal number. The second signal number is one more than the first signal number. By default, rtsig_signo is SIGRTMIN+10 (42), and the second signal number in this case would be 43.

rtsig_overflow_events, rtsig_overflow_test, and rtsig_overflow_threshold

The rtsig_overflow_events, rtsig_overflow_test, and rtsig_overflow_threshold directives define how the queue overflow is handled while using real-time signals. When overflow occurs, Nginx flushes the rtsig queue, then handles the switching of events between poll() and rtsig poll(), and handles all the unhandled events consecutively, while rtsig periodically drains the queues to prevent a new overflow. When the overflow is handled completely, Nginx switches to the rtsig method again.

The rtsig_overflow_events directive specifies the number of events to be passed via poll().

The rtsig_overflow_test directive specifies the number of events handled by poll(), after which, Nginx will drain the rtsig queue.

The rtsig_overflow_threshold directive works in Linux 2.4.x only. Before draining the rtsig queue, Nginx looks at the extent to which the queue has been filled up. The default is 1/10. rtsig_overflow_threshold 3 means a value of 1/3.

use

The `use` directive specifies the event-notification method that should be used (`kqueue`, epoll, and more). This is useful for platforms where multiple options are available. During the configuration time, the best method for event notification is selected automatically, so in most cases, you don't need to set this directive.

worker_connections

The `worker_connections` directive specifies the maximum number of simultaneous connections that can be opened by a worker process.

It should be kept in mind that this number includes all the connections and not just the client connections. Another consideration is that the actual number of simultaneous connections should not exceed the current limit on the maximum number of open files that can be changed by `worker_rlimit_nofile`.

Summary

In this chapter, we have looked at the configuration details of the two core modules of Nginx, that is, the `Main` and `Events` modules. These modules can't be opted out of, and you can't disable them. So, we went through each option and the suitable situations to use them.

In the next chapter, we will look at installing and configuring HTTP modules and the configuration options related to those modules.

3
Installing and Configuring HTTP Modules

In this chapter, we will explore the installation and configuration of standard HTTP modules. Standard HTTP modules are built into Nginx by default unless you disable them while running the configure script. The optional HTTP modules are only installed if you specify them explicitly while running `configure`. These modules deal with functionalities such as SSL, HTTP authentication, HTTP proxy, gzip compression, and many others. We will look at some optional HTTP modules in the next chapter.

All the configuration directives we have talked about so far and the ones that we will be discussing in this and the remaining chapters are specified in the `nginx.conf` file. The default location of this file is `/usr/local/conf/nginx.conf`.

Standard HTTP modules

As mentioned earlier, standard HTTP modules are built into Nginx by default unless you explicitly disable them. As the name suggests, these modules provide standard HTTP functionality to the web server. We will now have a look at some of the important standard HTTP modules.

The core module (HttpCoreModule)

The core module deals with the core HTTP features. This includes the protocol version, HTTP keepalive, location (different configurations based on URI), documents' roots, and so on. There are over 74 configuration directives and over 30 environment variables related to the HTTP Core module. We will discuss the most important ones briefly.

Explaining directives

The following is an explanation of some of the key core module directives.
This list is not exhaustive, and you can find the full list at `http://wiki.nginx.org/HttpCoreModule`.

server

The `server` directive defines the server context. It is defined as a `server {...}`
block in the configuration file. Each `server` block refers to a virtual server. You have
to specify a `listen` directive inside a `server` block to define the host IP and the port
for this virtual server. Alternatively, you can specify a `server_name` directive to
define all the hostnames of this virtual server.

```
server {
  server_name www.acme.com *.acme.com www.acme.org;
  ....
  ....
}
server {
  listen myserver.com:8001;
  ....
  ....
}
```

server_name

The `server_name` directive defines the name of the virtual server. It can contain
a list of hostnames, and the first one becomes the default name of the server.
The hostnames can be exact string literals, wildcards, regular expressions, or a
combination of all of these. You can also define an empty hostname as `""`. This
allows the processing of requests when the host HTTP header is empty.

The wildcard name can only use the asterisk (`*`) on the dot border and at the
beginning or ending of the name. For example, `*.example.com` is a valid name;
however, `ac*e.example.com` is an invalid name.

The regular expression server name can be any PCRE-compatible regular expression
that must start with `~`.

```
server_name ~^www\d+\.acme\.org$
```

If you specify the environment variable `$hostname` in this directive, the hostname
of the machine is used.

listen

The `listen` directive specifies the `listen` address of the server. The `listen` address can be a combination of an IP address and a port, hostname and port, or just a port.

```
server {
  listen 8001
  server_name www.acme.com *.acme.com www.acme.org
  ...
}
```

If no port is specified in the `listen` directive, the port 80 is used by default if the Nginx server is running as a `superuser`, otherwise the port 8000 is used.

Nginx can also listen on a UNIX socket using the following syntax:

```
listen unix:/var/lock/nginx
```

IPv6 addresses can be specified using the [] brackets:

```
listen [::]:80
listen [2001:db8::1]
```

Specifying an IPv6 address can enable the IPv4 address as well. In the first of the preceding examples, when you enable the `[::]:80` address, binding port 80 using IPv6 in the `listen` directive, the IPv4 port 80 is also enabled by default in Linux.

The `listen` directive accepts several parameters as well; a couple of important ones are stated in the following paragraphs.

SSL

The `listen` parameter allows you to specify that the connection accepted on this `listen` address will work in the SSL mode.

default_server

The `default_server` parameter sets the `listen` address as the default location. If none of the `listen` addresses have a default specification, the first `listen` declaration becomes the default. For an HTTP request, Nginx tests the request's header field, `Host`, to determine which server the request should be routed. If its value does not match any server name or the request does not contain this header field at all, Nginx will route the request to the default server.

```
listen  8001
listen  443 default_server ssl
```

The `ssl` option specifies that all connections on this address should work with SSL. The `ssl` option will only work if the server was compiled using SSL support.

There are other parameters of the `listen` directive that correspond to the `listen` and `bind` system calls. For example, you can modify the send and receive buffers of the listening socket by providing the `rcvbuf` and `sndbuf` parameters. You can read about them in more detail in the official documentation at `http://nginx.org/en/docs/http/ngx_http_core_module.html`.

location

The `location` directive is a server context configuration. There can be several location configuration blocks inside the `server` block, each referring to a unique URI within that server. It is one of the most important and widely used directives, which allows you to specify a configuration based on a URI. A location matching the user request URI will result in that specific configuration block to be the handler of user request. You have a lot of flexibility in how you want to specify the configuration. This can be a string literal or a regular expression. The regular expressions can be used to do a case-sensitive (prefixed with ~) or a case-insensitive comparison (prefixed with ~*). You can also disable the regular expression matching by prefixing the string with ^~.

The order of matching is as follows:

1. First, string literals with = are evaluated, and the searching stops on a match.
2. Remaining strings are matched; a match encountering ^~ also stops the search. Among all the non-regular-expression strings, the one with the longest matched prefix is chosen.
3. Regular expressions are searched in the order in which they appear in the `nginx.conf` file.
4. In case there are two matches, one from a regular expression and one from a string, the string is used.

    ```
    location = / matches only /
    location / matches any URI
    location ~/index matches a lower case /index as a subsring in any
       position
    ```

It does not matter in which order the configurations are defined. They will always be evaluated in the order mentioned previously.

```
location ^~/index/main.jpg
location ~^/index/.*\.jpg$
```

In the example, a URI such as `/index/main.jpg` will select the first rule even though both the patterns match. This is due to the `^~` prefix, which disables regular expression search.

It is also possible to define named locations with `@`, which are for internal use. For example:

```
location @internalerror (
  proxy_pass http://myserver/internalerror.html
)
```

You can then use the `@internalerror` in another configuration, that is:

```
location / (
  error_page /500.html @internalerror;
)
```

server_names_hash_bucket_size

Nginx stores static data in hash tables for quick access. There is a hash table maintained for each set of static data, such as server names. The identical names go into a hash bucket, and the `server_names_hash_bucket_size` parameter controls the size of a hash bucket in the server name hash table.

This parameter (and other `hash_bucket_size` parameters) should be a multiple of the processor's cache line size. This allows for an optimized search within a hash bucket ensuring that any entry can be found in a maximum of two memory reads. On Linux, you can find the cache line size as follows:

```
$ getconf LEVEL1_DCACHE_LINESIZE
```

server_names_hash_max_size

The `server_names_hash_max_size` directive specifies the maximum size of the hash table, which contains the server names. The size of the hash table calculated using the `server_names_hash_bucket_size` parameter cannot exceed this value. The default value is 512.

```
http {
  ...
  ...
  server_names_hash_bucket_size 128;
  server_names_hash_max_size 1024;
  server {
  ...
  ...
  }
}
```

tcp_nodelay/tcp_nopush

The `tcp_nodelay` and `tcp_nopush` directives allow you to control the socket settings of `tcp_nodelay` and `tcp_nopush` or `tcp_nocork` for Linux. `tcp_nodelay` is useful for servers that send frequent small bursts of packets without caring about the response. This directive essentially disables the Nagle algorithm on the TCP/IP socket. `tcp_nopush` or `tcp_nocork` will only have an effect if you use the `sendfile()` kernel option.

sendfile

The `sendfile` directive activates or deactivates the usage of Linux kernel's `sendfile()`. This offers significant performance benefits to applications such as web servers that need to efficiently transfer files. A web server spends much of its time transferring files stored on a disk to a network connection connected to a client running a web browser. Typically, this includes the `read()` and `write()` calls, which require context switching and data copying to and from user or kernel buffers. The `sendfile` system call allows Nginx to copy files from the disk to the socket using the fast track `sendfile()`, which stays within the kernel space. As of Linux 2.6.22, if you want to use the Aio with direct I/O (O_DIRECT) you should turn off `sendfile`. This can be more efficient if the web server serves large files (> 4 MB). In FreeBSD before 5.2.1 and Nginx 0.8.12, you must disable `sendfile` support as well.

sendfile_max_chunk

When set to a nonzero value, the `sendfile_max_chunk` directive limits the amount of data that can be transferred in a single `sendfile()` call.

root

`root` specifies the document root for the requests by appending a path to the request. For example, with the following configuration:

```
location  /images/ {
  root  /var/www;
}
```

A request for `/web/logo.gif` will return the file `/var/www/images/logo.gif`.

resolver/resolver_timeout

This allows you to specify the DNS server address or name. You can also define the timeout for name resolution, for example:

```
resolver 192.168.220.1;
resolver_timeout 2s;
```

aio

The `aio` directive allows Nginx to use the POSIX `aio` support in Linux. This asynchronous I/O mechanism allows multiple nonblocking reads and writes.

```
location /audio {
  aio on;
  directio 512;
  output_buffers 1 128k;
}
```

On Linux this will disable the `sendfile` support. In FreeBSD before 5.2.1 and Nginx 0.8.12, you must disable the `sendfile` support.

```
location /audio {
  aio on;
  sendfile off;
}
```

As of FreeBSD 5.2.1 and Nginx 0.8.12, you can use it with `sendfile`.

alias

The `alias` directive is similar to the `root` directive with a subtle difference. When you define an alias for a location, the alias path is searched instead of the actual location. This is slightly different from the root directive where the root path is appended to the location. For example:

```
location  /img/ {
  alias  /var/www/images/;
}
```

A request for `/img/logo.gif` will instruct Nginx to serve the file `/var/www/images/logo.gif`.

Aliases can also be used in a location specified by a regular expression.

error_page

The `error_page` directive allows you to show error pages based on error code. For example:

```
error_page   404           /404.html;
error_page   502 503 504   /50x.html;
```

It is possible to show a different error code instead of the original error. It is also possible to specify a script like a php file (which in turn generates the content of the error page). This can allow you to write one generic error handler that creates a customized page depending on the error code and type:

```
error_page 404 =200 /empty.gif;
error_page 500 =errors.php;
```

If there is no need to change the URL in the browser during redirection, it is possible to redirect the processing of error pages to a named location:

```
location / (
  error_page 404 @errorhandler;
)
location @ errorhandler (
  proxy_pass http://backend/errors.php;
)
```

keepalive_disable, keepalive_timeout, and keepalive_ requests

The `keepalive_disable` directive allows you to disable the HTTP `keepalive` for certain browsers.

`keepalive_timeout` assigns the timeout for the `keepalive` connections with the client. The server will close connections after this time. You can also specify a zero value to disable the keepalive for client connections. This adds an HTTP header Keep-Alive: timeout=time to the response.

`keepalive_requests` parameter determines how many client requests will be served through a single keepalive connection. Once this limit is reached the connection is closed, and new keepalive session will be initiated.

Controlling access (HttpAccessModule)

The `HttpAccessModule` allows IP-based access control. You can specify both IPv4 and IPv6 addresses. Another alternative is using the GeoIP module.

Rules are checked according to the order of their declaration. There are two directives called `allow` and `deny` which control the access. The first rule that matches a particular address or a set of addresses is the one that is obeyed.

```
location / {
  deny    192.168.1.1;
  allow   192.168.1.0/24;
  allow   10.1.1.0/16;
```

```
    allow   2620:100:e000::8001;
    deny    all;
}
```

In this example access is granted to the networks 10.1.1.0/16 and 192.168.1.0/24 with the exception of the address 192.168.1.1, which is denied access together with all the other addresses as defined by the `deny all` rule that is matched last in this location block. In addition, it allows one specific IPv6 address. All others would be denied.

The order is of utmost importance. The rules are interpreted according to the order. So, if you move `deny all` to the top of the list, all requests will be denied because that's the first rule that is encountered, and therefore, it takes precedence.

Authenticating users (HttpBasicAuthModule)

You can use the `HttpBasicAuthModule` to protect your site or parts of it with a username and password based on HTTP Basic authentication. It is the simplest technique for enforcing access controls to web resources because it doesn't require cookies, session identifier, and login pages. Rather, HTTP Basic authentication uses static, standard HTTP headers, which mean that no handshakes have to be done in anticipation.

The following is an example configuration:

```
location / {
  auth_basic              "Registered Users Only";
  auth_basic_user_file  htpasswd;
}
```

Explaining directives

Now let us look at some of the important directives of this module.

auth_basic

This `auth_basic` directive includes testing the name and password with HTTP Basic authentication. The assigned value is used as authentication realm.

auth_basic_user_file

The `auth_basic_user_file` directive sets the password filename for the authentication realm. The path is relative to the directory of the Nginx configuration file.

The format of the file is as follows:

```
user:pass
user2:pass2:comment
user3:pass3
```

Passwords must be encoded by the function crypt (3). You can use PLAIN, MD5, SSHA, and SHA1 encryption methods. If you have Apache installed on your system, you can use the `htpasswd` utility to generate the `htpasswd` file.

This file should be readable by Nginx worker processes, running from an unprivileged user.

Load balancing (HttpUpstreamModule)

The `HttpUpstreamModule` allows simple load balancing based on a variety of techniques such as Round-robin, weight, IP address, and so on to a collection of upstream servers.

Example:

```
upstream servers  {
  server server1.example.com weight=5;
  server server2.example.com:8080;
  server unix:/tmp/server3;
}
server {
  location / {
    proxy_pass  http://servers;
  }
}
```

Explaining directives

Some of the important directives of the `HttpUpstreamModule` are as follows:

ip_hash

The `ip_hash` directive causes requests to be distributed between servers based on the IP address of the client.

The key for the hash is the IP address (IPv4 or IPv6) of the client. This method guarantees that the client request will always be transferred to the same server. If the server is not available, the request is transferred to another server.

You can combine `ip_hash` and `weight` based methods. If one of the servers needs to be taken offline, you must mark that server as `down`.

For example:

```
upstream backend {
  ip_hash;
  server    server1.example.com weight=2;
  server    server2.example.com;
  server    server3.example.com  down;
  server    server4.example.com;
}
```

server

The `server` directive is used to specify the name of the upstream server. It is possible to use a domain name, address, port, or UNIX socket. If the domain name resolves to several addresses, all are used.

This directive accepts several parameters, which are given as follows:

- `weight`: This sets the weight of the server. If it is not set, weight is equal to one.

- `max_fails`: This is the number of unsuccessful attempts at communicating with the server within the time period `fail_timeout` after which it is considered `down`. If it is not set, only one attempt is made. A value of `0` turns off this check. What is considered a failure is defined by `proxy_next_upstream` or `fastcgi_next_upstream` (except `http_404` errors, which do not count toward `max_fails`).

- `fail_timeout`: The time period within which failed attempts to connect to an upstream server are attempted before the server is considered `down`. It is also the time for which the server will be considered inoperative (before another attempt is made). The default value is 10 seconds.

- `down`: This parameter marks the server as offline.

If you use only one upstream server, Nginx will ignore the `max_fails` and `fail_timeout` parameters. This may cause your request to be lost if the upstream server is not available. You can use the same server name several times to simulate retries.

upstream

The `upstream` directive describes a set of upstream or backend servers to which the requests are sent. These are the servers that can be used in the directives `proxy_pass` and `fastcgi_pass` as a single entity. Each of the defined servers can be on different ports. You can also specify servers listening on local sockets.

Servers can be assigned different weights. If it is not specified, the weight is equal to one.

```
upstream servers {
  server server1.example.com weight=5;
  server 127.0.0.1:8080        max_fails=3  fail_timeout=30s;
  server unix:/tmp/localserver;
}
```

Requests are distributed according to the servers in the Round-robin manner with respect to the server weight.

For example, for every seven requests given previously, their distribution will be as follows: five requests will be sent to `server1.example.com` and one request each to the second and the third server. If there is an error in connecting to the server, the request is sent to the next server. In the previous example, there will be three tries within 30 s for server 2 in case of a failure before the request is forwarded to server 3.

Acting as a proxy (HttpProxyModule)

The `HttpProxyModule` allows Nginx to act as a proxy and pass requests to another server.

```
location / {
  proxy_pass         http://app.localhost:8000;
}
```

Note when using the `HttpProxyModule` (or even when using FastCGI), the entire client request will be buffered in Nginx before being passed on to the proxy server.

Explaining directives

Some of the important directives of the `HttpProxyModule` are as follows:

proxy_pass

The `proxy_pass` directive sets the address of the proxy server and the URI to which the location will be mapped. The address may be given as a hostname or an address and port, for example:

```
proxy_pass http://localhost:8000/uri/;
```

Or, the address may be given as an UNIX socket path:

```
proxy_pass http://unix:/path/to/backend.socket:/uri/;
```

`path` is given after the word `unix` between two colons.

You can use the `proxy_pass` directive to forward headers from the client request to the proxied server.

```
proxy_set_header Host $host;
```

While passing requests, Nginx replaces the location in the URI with the location specified by the `proxy_pass` directive.

If inside the proxied location, URI is changed by the `rewrite` directive and this configuration will be used to process the request. For example:

```
location  /name/ {
    rewrite      /name/([^/] +)  /users?name=$1  break;
    proxy_pass   http://127.0.0.1;
}
```

A request URI is passed to the proxy server after normalization as follows:

- Double slashes are replaced by a single slash
- Any references to current directory like "./" are removed
- Any references to the previous directory like "../" are removed.

If `proxy_pass` is specified without a URI (for example in "`http://example.com/request`", `/request` is the URI part), the request URI is passed to the server in the same form as sent by a client.

```
location /some/path/ {
    proxy_pass http://127.0.0.1;
}
```

If you need the proxy connection to an upstream server group to use SSL, your `proxy_pass` rule should use `https://` and you will also have to set your SSL port explicitly in the upstream definition. For example:

```
upstream https-backend {
    server 10.220.129.20:443;
}

server {
    listen 10.220.129.1:443;
    location / {
        proxy_pass https://backend-secure;
    }
}
```

proxy_pass_header

The `proxy_pass_header` directive allows transferring header lines forbidden for response.

```
For example:
location / {
  proxy_pass_header X-Accel-Redirect;
}
```

proxy_connect_timeout

The `proxy_connect_timeout` directive sets a connection timeout to the upstream server. You can't set this timeout value to be more than 75 seconds. Please remember that this is not the response timeout, but only a connection timeout.

This is not the time until the server returns the pages which is configured through `proxy_read_timeout` directive. If your upstream server is up but hanging, this statement will not help as the connection to the server has been made.

proxy_next_upstream

The `proxy_next_upstream` directive determines in which cases the request will be transmitted to the next server:

- `error`: An error occurred while connecting to the server, sending a request to it, or reading its response
- `timeout`: The timeout occurred during the connection with the server, transferring the request, or while reading the response from the server
- `invalid_header`: The server returned an empty or incorrect response
- `http_500`: The server responded with code 500
- `http_502`: The server responded with code 502
- `http_503`: The server responded with code 503
- `http_504`: The server responded with code 504
- `http_404`: The server responded with code 404
- `off`: Disables request forwarding

Transferring the request to the next server is only possible if there is an error sending the request to one of the servers. If the request sending was interrupted due to an error or some other reason, the transfer of request will not take place.

proxy_redirect

The `proxy_redirect` directive allows you to manipulate the HTTP redirection by replacing the text in the response from the upstream server. Specifically, it replaces text in the `Location` and `Refresh` headers.

The HTTP `Location` header field is returned in response from a proxied server for the following reasons:

- To indicate that a resource has moved temporarily or permanently.
- To provide information about the location of a newly created resource. This could be the result of an HTTP PUT.

Let us suppose that the proxied server returned the following:

```
Location: http://localhost:8080/images/new_folder
```

If you have the `proxy_redirect` directive set to the following:

```
proxy_redirect http://localhost:8080/images/ http://xyz/;
```

The `Location` text will be rewritten to be similar to the following:

```
Location: http://xyz/new_folder/.
```

It is possible to use some variables in the redirected address:

```
proxy_redirect http://localhost:8000/ http://$location:8000;
```

You can also use regular expressions in this directive:

```
proxy_redirect ~^(http://[^:]+):\d+(/.+)$ $1$2;
```

The value `off` disables all the `proxy_redirect` directives at its level.

```
proxy_redirect off;
```

proxy_set_header

The `proxy_set_header` directive allows you to redefine and add new HTTP headers to the request sent to the proxied server.

You can use a combination of static text and variables as the value of the `proxy_set_header` directive.

By default, the following two headers will be redefined:

```
proxy_set_header Host $proxy_host;
proxy_set_header Connection Close;
```

You can forward the original `Host` header value to the server as follows:

```
proxy_set_header Host $http_host;
```

However, if this header is absent in the client request, nothing will be transferred.

It is better to use the variable `$host`; its value is equal to the request header `Host` or to the basic name of the server in case the header is absent from the client request.

```
proxy_set_header Host $host;
```

You can transmit the name of the server together with the port of the proxied server:

```
proxy_set_header Host $host:$proxy_port;
```

If you set the value to an empty string, the header is not passed to the upstream proxied server. For example, if you want to disable the gzip compression on upstream, you can do the following:

```
proxy_set_header  Accept-Encoding   "";
```

proxy_store

The `proxy_store` directive sets the path in which upstream files are stored, with paths corresponding to the directives `alias` or `root`. The `off` directive value disables local file storage. Please note that `proxy_store` is different from `proxy_cache`. It is just a method to store proxied files on disk. It may be used to construct cache-like setups (usually involving error_page-based fallback). This `proxy_store` directive parameter is `off` by default. The value can contain a mix of static strings and variables.

```
proxy_store    /data/www$uri;
```

The modification date of the file will be set to the value of the `Last-Modified` header in the response. A response is first written to a temporary file in the path specified by `proxy_temp_path` and then renamed. It is recommended to keep this location path and the path to store files the same to make sure it is a simple renaming instead of creating two copies of the file.

Example:

```
location /images/ {
  root                /data/www;
  error_page          404 = @fetch;
}

location /fetch {
  internal;
  proxy_pass          http://backend;
```

```
    proxy_store          on;
    proxy_store_access   user:rw  group:rw  all:r;
    proxy_temp_path      /data/temp;
    alias                /data/www;
}
```

In this example, `proxy_store_access` defines the access rights of the created file.

In the case of an error `404`, the fetch internal location proxies to a remote server and stores the local copies in the `/data/temp` folder.

proxy_cache

The `proxy_cache` directive either turns off caching when you use the value `off` or sets the name of the cache. This name can then be used subsequently in other places as well. Let's look at the following example to enable caching on the Nginx server:

```
http {
    proxy_cache_path  /var/www/cache levels=1:2 keys_zone=my-
        cache:8m max_size=1000m inactive=600m;
    proxy_temp_path /var/www/cache/tmp;


    server {
      location / {
        proxy_pass http://example.net;
        proxy_cache my-cache;
        proxy_cache_valid  200 302  60m;
        proxy_cache_valid  404      1m;
      }
    }
}
```

The previous example creates a named cache called `my-cache`. It sets up the validity of the cache for response codes `200` and `302` to `60m`, and for `404` to `1m`, respectively.

The cached data is stored in the `/var/www/cache` folder. The `levels` parameter sets the number of subdirectory levels in the cache. You can define up to three levels.

The name of `key_zone` is followed by an inactive interval. All the inactive items in `my-cache` will be purged after `600m`. The default value for inactive intervals is 10 minutes.

Compressing content (HttpGzipModule)

The `HttpGzipModule` allows for on-the-fly gzip compression.

```
gzip                on;
gzip_min_length     1000;
gzip_proxied        expired no-cache no-store private auth;
gzip_types          text/plain application/xml;
```

The achieved compression ratio, computed as the ratio between the original and the compressed response size, is available via the variable `$gzip_ratio`.

Explaining directives

Some of the important directives of the `HttpGzipModule` are as follows:

gzip

The `gzip` directive enables or disables gzip compression.

gzip_buffers

The `gzip_buffers` directive assigns the number and size of the buffers in which the compressed response will be stored. If unset, the size of one buffer is equal to the size of the page; depending on the platform, this is either 4K or 8K.

gzip_comp_level

The `gzip_comp_level` directive sets a gzip compression level of a response. The compression level, between 1 and 9, where 1 is the least compression (fastest) and 9 is the most compression (slowest).

gzip_disable

The `gzip_disable` directive disables gzip compression for browsers or user agents matching the given regular expression. For example, to disable gzip compression for Internet Explorer 6 use:

```
gzip_disable    "msie6";
```

This is a useful setting to have since some browsers such as MS Internet Explorer 6 don't handle the compressed response correctly.

gzip_http_version

The `gzip_http_version` directive turns gzip compression on or off depending on the HTTP request version, which is 1.0 or 1.1.

gzip_min_length

The `gzip_min_length` directive sets the minimum length, in bytes, of the response that will be compressed. Responses shorter than this byte length will not be compressed. Length is determined from the `Content-Length` header.

gzip_proxied

The `gzip_proxied` directive enables or disables compression for proxied requests. The proxied requests are identified through the `Via` HTTP header. This header informs the server of proxies through which the request was sent. Depending on various HTTP headers, we can enable or disable the compression for proxied requests as follows:

- `off`: This disables compression for requests having a `Via` header
- `expired`: This enables compression if a response header includes the field `Expires` with a value that disables caching
- `no-cache`: This enables compression if the `Cache-Control` header is set to `no-cache`
- `no-store`: This enables compression if the `Cache-Control` header is set to `no-store`
- `private`: This enables compression if the `Cache-Control` header is set to `private`
- `no_last_modified`: This enables compression if `Last-Modified` isn't set
- `no_etag`: This enables compression if there is no `ETag` header
- `auth`: This enables compression if there is an `Authorization` header
- `any`: This enables compression for all proxied requests

gzip_types

The `gzip_types` directive enables compression for additional MIME types besides text or html. `text/html` is always compressed.

Controlling logging (HttpLogModule)

The `HttpLogModule` controls how Nginx logs the requests for resources, for example:

```
access_log  /var/log/nginx/access.log  gzip  buffer=32k;
```

Please note that this does not include logging errors.

Explaining directives

Some of the important directives of `HttpLogModule` are the following.

access_log

The `access_log` directive sets the path, format, and buffer size for the access logfile. Using `off` as the value disables logging at the current level. If the format is not indicated, it defaults to `combined`. The size of the buffer must not exceed the size of the atomic record for writing into the disk file. This size is not limited for FreeBSD 3.0-6.0. If you specify gzip, the log is compressed before it's written to the disk. The default buffer size is 64K with compression level as 1.

The atomic size that can be written is called `PIPE_BUF`. The capacity of a pipe buffer varies across systems.

Mac OS X, for example, uses a capacity of 16,384 bytes by default but can switch to 65,336 byte capacities if large writes are made to the pipe. Or it will switch to a capacity of a single system page if too much kernel memory is already being used by pipe buffers (see `xnu/bsd/sys/pipe.h` and `xnu/bsd/kern/sys_pipe.c`; since these are from FreeBSD, the same behavior may happen here too).

According to the Linux pipe(7) man page, pipe capacity is 65,536 bytes since Linux 2.6.11 and a single system page prior to that (for example, 4096 bytes on 32-bit x86 systems). The buffer for each pipe can be changed using fcntl system call to the maximum of `/proc/sys/fs/pipe-max-size`.

log_format

The `log_format` directive describes the format of a log entry. You can use general variables in the format as well as variables that exist only at the moment of writing into the log. An example of log_format is as follows:

```
log_format gzip '$msec $request $remote-addr $status $bytes_sent';
```

You can specify the format of a log entry by specifying what information should be logged. Some of the options you can specify are as follows:

- `$body_bytes_sent`: This is the number of bytes transmitted to the client minus the response headers
- `$bytes_sent`: This is the number of bytes transmitted to the client
- `$connection`: This is the number of connections
- `$msec`: This is the current time at the moment of writing the log entry (microsecond accuracy)
- `$pipe`: This is p if request was pipelined

- `$request_length`: This is the length of the body of the request
- `$request_time`: This is the time it took Nginx to work on the request, in seconds, with millisecond precision
- `$status`: This is the status of the answer
- `$time_iso8601`: This is the time in ISO 8601 format, for example, 2011-03-21T18:52:25+03
- `$time_local`: This is the local time in common log format

Setting response headers (HttpHeadersModule)

The `HttpHeadersModule` allows setting arbitrary HTTP headers.

Explaining directives

Some of the important directives of the `HttpHeadersModule` are the following:

add_header

The `add_header` directive adds a header to the header list of the response when the response code is 200, 201, 204, 206, 301, 302, 303, 304, or 307. The value can contain variables and can contain negative or positive time value.

Note that you should not use this directive to replace or override the value of a header. The headers specified with this directive are simply appended to the header list.

expires

The `expires` directive is used to set the `Expires` and `Cache-Control` headers in the response. You can set the value to `off` to leave these headers as it is. The time in this field is computed as a sum of the current time and the time specified in the directive. If the modified parameter is used, time is computed as a sum of the file's modification time and the time specified in the directive.

- `epoch`: This sets the `Expires` header to the absolute value of `1 January, 1970 00:00:01 GMT`.
- `max`: This sets the `Expires` header to `31 December 2037 23:59:59 GMT`, and the `Cache-Control` header to 10 years.

You can specify a time interval using @:

```
@5h40m
```

The contents of the `Cache-Control` header depend on the sign of the specified time. A negative value of time sets it to `no-cache`. A positive value sets it to time in seconds.

The following is an example configuration:

```
expires    12h;
expires    modified +14h;
expires    @5h;
expires    0;
expires    -1;
expires    epoch;
add_header X-Name example.org
```

Rewriting requests (HttpRewriteModule)

The `HttpRewriteModule` is used to change request URIs using regular expressions, redirect the client, and select different configurations based on conditions and variable values. In order to use this module, you should compile Nginx with PCRE support.

The processing of the directives starts at the server level. After this, the location block matching the request is searched and any rewrite directives there are executed. If this processing results in further rewrites, a new location block is search for the changed URI. This cycle continues 10 times before the server throws the `500` error.

Explaining directives

Some of the important directives of the `HttpRewriteModule` are the following:

break

The `break` directive stops the processing of any other rewrite block directives in the current block.

```
if ($slow) {
  limit_rate  10k;
  break;
}
```

if

The `if` directive checks a condition. If the condition evaluates to `true`, the code indicated in the curly braces is carried out and the request is processed in accordance with the configuration within the following block. The configuration inside the `if` block is inherited from the previous level.

Following are considered to be valid conditions.

- The name of a variable is a condition. The condition evaluates to `false` if the variable contains an empty string `""` or a `0`.

- Using comparison operator with the variable to compare it to another variable or a string.

- Matching a variable against a regular expression using `~`, `*~`, or `!~` operator. `*~` is used for case-insensitive comparison, while `!~` is a not-equals operator.

- You can check for the existence of a file using the `-f` or `!-f` operators (similar to BASH tests).

- Checking for the existence of a directory using `-d` or `!-d`.

- Checking for the existence of a file, directory, or symbolic link using `-e` or `!-e`.

- Checking whether a file is executable using `-x` or `!-x`.

By placing part of a regular expression inside round brackets or parentheses, you can group that part of the regular expression together. This allows you to apply a quantifier to the entire group or to restrict alternation to part of the regular expression. These parts can be accessed in the `$1` to `$9` variables.

Example:

```
if ($http_user_agent ~ MSIE) {
  rewrite ^(.*)$  /msie/$1  break;
}
if ($http_cookie ~* "val=([^;] +)(?:;|$)" ) {
  set $val $1;
}
if ($request_method = GET ) {
  return 405;
}
if ($args ~ post=140){
  rewrite ^ http://acme.com/ permanent
}
```

return

The `return` directive stops execution and returns a status code. It is possible to use any HTTP return code ranging in number from `0` to `999`.

If you want to terminate the connection and don't want to send any headers in response, use the return code `444`.

rewrite

The `rewrite` directive does the actual rewrite and changes URI according to the regular expression and the replacement string. Directives are carried out in the order of definition in the configuration file. The `flag` parameter makes it possible to stop the rewriting process in the current block.

If the replacement string begins with `http://`, the client will be redirected and any further rewrite directives will be terminated.

The value of the `flag` parameter can be one of the following:

- `last`: This completes the processing of current rewrite directives and searches for a new block that matches the rewritten URI
- `break`: This stops the rewriting process in the current block
- `redirect`: This returns a temporary redirect with the code `302`, and is used if a replacement string does not start with `http://` or `https://`
- `permanent`: This returns a permanent redirect with code `301`

Note that outside location blocks, `last` and `break` are effectively the same.

Example:

```
rewrite  ^(/media/.*)/video/(.*)\..*$  $1/mp3/$2.avi last;
rewrite  ^(/media/.*)/audio/(.*)\..*$  $1/mp3/$2.ra break;
return 403;
```

But if we place these directives in the `location` block, it is necessary to replace the flag `last` by `break`, otherwise Nginx will hit the 10-cycle limit and return error `500`:

```
location /download/ {
  rewrite  ^(/media/.*)/video/(.*)\..*$  $1/mp3/$2.avi  break;
  rewrite  ^(/media/.*)/audio/(.*)\..*$  $1/mp3/$2.ra   break;
  return   403;
}
```

If there are arguments in the replacement string, the rest of the request arguments are appended to them. To avoid having them appended, place a question mark as the last character:

```
rewrite  ^/pages/(.*)$  /show?page=$1?  last;
```

Note that for curly braces ({ and }), as they are used both in regex and for block control, to avoid conflicts, regex with curly braces are to be enclosed with double quotes (or single quotes). For example, to rewrite URLs such as `/users/123456` to `/path/to/users/12/1234/123456.html`, use the following (note the quotes):

```
rewrite  "/users/([0-9]{2})([0-9]{2})([0-9]{2})"
   /path/to/users/$1/$1$2/$1$2$3.html;
```

If you specify a `?` at the end of a rewrite, Nginx will drop the original query string. A good use case is when using `$request_uri`, you should specify the `?` at the end of the rewrite to avoid Nginx doubling the query string.

An example of using `$request_uri` in a rewrite from `www.acme.com` to `acme.com`:

```
server {
  server_name www.acme.com;
  rewrite ^ http://acme.com$request_uri? permanent;
}
```

Also, rewrite operates only on paths, not on parameters. To rewrite a URL with parameters to another URL, use the following instead:

```
if ($args ~ post=200){
  rewrite ^ http://acme.com/new-address.html?;
}
```

rewrite_log

The `rewrite_log` directive enables the logging of information about rewrites to the error log at notice level.

set

The `set` directive establishes the value for the variable indicated. It is possible to use text, variables, and their combination as the value.

You can use set to define a new variable. Note that you can't set the value of a `$http_xxx` header variable.

uninitialized_variable_warn

The `uninitialized_variable_warn` directive enables or disables warnings of variables that are not initialized.

Interacting with FastCGI (HttpFastcgiModule)

The `HttpFastcgiModule` allows Nginx to interact with the FastCGI processes (that is, PHP) and controls which parameters will be passed to the process.

Example:

```
location / {
  fastcgi_pass    localhost:9090;
  fastcgi_index   index.php;
   fastcgi_param   SCRIPT_FILENAME
    $document_root/php/$fastcgi_script_name;
  fastcgi_param   QUERY_STRING      $query_string;
  fastcgi_param   REQUEST_METHOD    $request_method;
  fastcgi_param   CONTENT_TYPE      $content_type;
  fastcgi_param   CONTENT_LENGTH    $content_length;
}
```

The name of the FastCGI server is provided in the `fastcgi_pass` parameter. This name can be an IP address or a domain name with a port. This can also be an UNIX domain socket.

If you want to pass a parameter to the FastCGI server, you use the `fastcgi_param` parameter. The value of this parameter can be a static value, a variable, or a combination of both.

Following is a minimum configuration for PHP:

```
fastcgi_param SCRIPT_FILENAME /php$fastcgi_script_name;
fastcgi_param QUERY_STRING    $query_string;
```

Simple caching (HttpMemcachedModule)

You can use this module to perform simple caching using memcached. Memcached is an in-memory, key-value store for small chunks of arbitrary data (strings, objects) from the results of database calls, API calls, or page rendering.

Example:

```
server {
  location / {
    set $memcached_key $uri$args;
    memcached_pass      http://mem-server:1211
    default_type        text/html;
      error_page          404 502 504 @error;
  }
```

```
location @error {
  proxy_pass http://backend;
}
}
```

Explaining directives

Some of the important directives of the `HttpMemcachedModule` are as follows:

memcached_pass

The `memcached_pass` directive specifies the memcached server name as an IP or domain name. It can also contain a port. If the domain name translates into various addresses, all of them are tried in the Round-robin fashion.

memcached_connect_timeout

The `memcached_connect_timeout` directive is the timeout for connecting to the memcached server. The time of the timeout usually can be `75s` at maximum. The default value is `60s`.

memcached_read_timeout

The `memcached_read_timeout` directive is the timeout for reading keys from the memcached server. This time is measured between two successive reads, and if the memcached server does not respond, the timeout occurs. The default value is `60s`.

memcached_send_timeout

The `memcached_send_timeout` directive is the timeout for sending a request to the memcached server. A timeout is only set between two successive write operations and not for the transmission of the whole request. If a memcached server does not receive anything within this time, a connection is closed.

memcached_buffer_size

The `memcached_buffer_size` directive is the receive or send buffer size in bytes. It sets the size of the buffer used for reading a response received from the memcached server. A response is passed to a client synchronously and immediately when it is received. Default value is `4K` or `8K`.

memcached_next_upstream

Which failure conditions should cause the request to be forwarded to another memcached upstream server? The answer is only when the value in `memcached_pass` is an upstream block with two or more servers.

Limiting requests (HttpLimitReqModule)

The `HttpLimitReqModule` allows limiting the request processing rate by key, in particular by the address. The limitation is done using the leaky bucket method. A counter associated with each address transmitting on a connection is incremented whenever the user sends a request and is decremented periodically. If the counter exceeds a threshold upon being incremented, Nginx delays the request.

The following is an example configuration:

```
http {
    limit_req_zone  $binary_remote_addr  zone=one:10m   rate=1r/s;

    ...

    server {

        ...

        location /search/ {
            limit_req   zone=one  burst=5;
        }
```

Explaining directives

Some of the important directives of the `HttpLimitReqModule` are as follows:

limit_req

The `limit_req` directive sets a shared memory zone and the maximum burst size of requests. Excessive requests are delayed until their number exceeds the maximum burst size in which case the request is terminated with an error `503` (Service Temporarily Unavailable). By default, the maximum burst size is equal to zero. For example, for the directive `limit_req_zone`:

```
$binary_remote_addr  zone=one:10m   rate=1r/s;
    server {
        location /search/ {
            limit_req   zone=one  burst=5;
        }
```

It allows a user no more than one request per second on average with bursts of no more than five requests.

If delaying excess requests within a burst is not necessary, you should use the option `nodelay`:

```
limit_req zone=one burst=5 nodelay;
```

limit_req_log_level

The `limit_req_log_level` directive controls the log level of the delayed or rejected requests. The log levels can be `info`, `notice`, `warn`, or `error`. The default log level is `error` for rejected requests. Delays are logged at the next lower level, for example when limit_req_log_level is set to "error", delayed requests are logged at "warn".

limit_req_zone

The `limit_req_zone` directive sets the name and parameters of a shared memory zone that keeps states for various keys. The state stores the current number of excessive requests in particular. The key is any nonempty value of the specified variable (empty values are not accounted). An example usage of this is as follows:

```
limit_req_zone $binary_remote_addr zone=myzone:20m rate=5r/s;
```

In this case, there is a 20 MB zone called `myzone`, and the average speed of queries for this zone is limited to 5 requests per second.

The sessions are tracked per user in this case. A 1 MB zone can hold approximately 16,000 states of 64 bytes. If the storage for a zone is exhausted, the server will return error `503` (Service Temporarily Unavailable) to all further requests.

The speed is set in requests per second or requests per minute. The rate must be an integer; so if you need to specify less than one request per second, say, one request every two seconds, you would specify it as `30r/m`.

Limiting connections (HttpLimitConnModule)

The `HttpLimitConnModule` makes it possible to limit the number of concurrent connections for a key such as an IP address.

An example configuration:

```
http {
    limit_conn_zone $binary_remote_addr zone=addr:10m;

    ...

    server {

        ...

        location /download/ {
            limit_conn addr 1;
        }
```

Explaining directives

Some of the important directives of `HttpLimitConnModule` are as follows:

limit_conn

The value of the `limit_conn` directive defines the limit of connection per zone. When this limit is exceeded, the server will return a status error `503` (Service Temporarily Unavailable) in reply to the request.

Multiple limit directives for different zones can be used in the same context. For example:

```
limit_conn_zone $binary_remote_addr zone=addr:10m;

server {
    location /download/ {
        limit_conn addr 1;
    }
```

This is allowed for only a single connection at a time per unique IP address.

limit_conn_zone

The `limit_conn_zone` directive sets the parameters for a zone that keeps the state for various keys. This state stores the current number of connections in particular. The key is the value of the specified variable. For example:

```
limit_conn_zone $binary_remote_addr zone=addr:10m;
```

Here, an IP address of the client serves as a key. If the storage for a zone is exhausted, the server will return error `503` (Service Temporarily Unavailable) to all further requests.

limit_conn_log_level

The `limit_conn_log_level` directive sets the error log level, which is used when a connection limit is reached. The default log level is `error`.

limit_conn_status

The `limit_conn_status` directive defines the response code when a limit is reached. The default value is `503` (Service Unavailable).

Summary

In this chapter we looked at several standard HTTP modules. These modules provide a very rich set of functionalities by default. You can disable these modules if you please at the time of configuration. However, they will be installed by default if you don't. The list of modules and their directives in this chapter is by no means exhaustive. Nginx's online documentation can provide you with more details.

In the next chapter we will look into some optional HTTP modules.

4
Installing Third-party Modules

In this chapter we will explore the installation of third-party modules. Third-party modules are developed by a vast variety of developers around the world and are hosted on various open source repositories such as GitHub and SourceForge. Some of these modules are well tested while others are not quite ready for production. These modules are not officially supported by Nginx developers and might have issues across different Nginx versions. In this chapter, we will talk about some of the most well-known Nginx modules. A bigger list of available options can be browsed on the Nginx website at `http://wiki.nginx.org/3rdPartyModules`.

All the configuration directives that we have discussed so far, and the ones that we will discuss in this and the remaining chapters, are specified in the `nginx.conf` file. The default location of the `nginx.conf` file is `/usr/local/conf/`.

Compiling third-party modules

None of the third-party modules that we will be covering in this chapter are distributed with the source code. You will have to download the source code and compile it by specifying its location while compiling Nginx. You can do that by specifying the `--add-module` parameters while running `configure`. For example, if you downloaded the module's source code present in `/opt/downloads`, you can compile it in the Nginx binary with the following code:

```
configure --add-module=/opt/downloads/module-folder
```

Some of these modules may have additional dependencies, which you will have to resolve. Please refer to the documentation of the module you are trying to install, to make sure you understand the consequences and dependencies of the module you are about to compile.

Communicating with PostgreSQL (ngx_postgres)

The Nginx PostgreSQL module is currently hosted at http://labs.frickle.com/ nginx_ngx_postgres/ and maintained by Frickle Labs. It is an upstream module that allows direct communication with the PostgreSQL database. The output of this module is in a custom binary format named **Resty DBD Stream (RDS)**.This module is useful if you want to directly connect Nginx to a PostgreSQL database. There can be several use-cases of why you would want to do that. You might want to serve pages by directly querying results from a table. You might also want to log things in a database or check certain conditions by querying a database table. Or you might want to authenticate a user from an upstream PostgreSQL database. For all such situations and more, the ngx_postgres module will be useful.

An example configuration is as follows:

```
http {
    upstream database {
        postgres_server   127.0.0.1 dbname=test
                          user=user password=password;
    }

    server {
        location / {
            postgres_pass    database;
            postgres_query   "select * from users";
        }
    }
}
```

Explaining directives

Some important directives of the ngx_postgres module are as follows:

postgres_server

The postgres_server directive sets the details of the database server. You can specify the hostname or IP address along with a port, username, and password.

An example configuration is as follows:

```
postgres_server   127.0.0.1 dbname=test user=test password=test;
```

postgres_keepalive

The `postgres_keepalive` directive is used to configure `keepalive` parameters. The syntax is as follows:

```
postgres_keepalive off | max=count [mode=single|multi]
[overflow=ignore|reject]
default: max=10 mode=single overflow=ignore
```

Here, the `max` parameter determines the maximum number of `keepalive` connections. The `mode` parameter has two possible values, `multi` and `single`. The `single` mode means that the connection pool will not differentiate between multiple `postgres_server` definitions in the current block and will apply to all of them, that is, you have one pool for all the `postgres_server` definitions. In the `multi` mode, the pool will re-use connections that have identical server hostnames and ports. The default value is `single`. The `overflow` option specifies what to do when the connection pool is already full and a new database connection is required. Either `reject` or `ignore` can be specified. In case of `reject`, it will reject the current request and return the **503 Service Unavailable** error page. On using `ignore`, this module will create a new database connection.

postgres_pass

The `postgres_pass` directive holds the name of the upstream block that contains the PostgreSQL connection's configurations. It can also contain variables.

postgres_query

The `postgres_query` directive is used to specify a PostgreSQL query. If an HTTP method such as GET, POST, PUT, or DELETE is specified, the query is used only for the specified methods; otherwise, it will run for all the methods. A query can contain variables and you can specify multiple query directives in one location. An example configuration is as follows:

```
postgres_query    GET POST   "SELECT * FROM employees";
```

postgres_rewrite

The `postgres_rewrite` directive should be used to send a specific response code when a condition is met. The condition can be one of the following:

- `no_changes`: This is the condition when no rows are affected by the query
- `changes`: This is the condition when at least one row is affected by the query
- `no_rows`: This is the condition when no rows are returned in the result set
- `rows`: This is the condition when at least one row is returned in the result set

If you want to send the original response body to the client, prefix the code with = as shown in the following example configuration:

```
postgres_rewrite  no_rows =403;
```

postgres_output

The `postgres_output` directive determines the output type of the response. The possible values are `rds`, `text`, `binary`, `value`, and `none`. The `none` value is used when you don't want any output. `value` is used when you want a single value as an output in the text format. All response types set the appropriate HTTP header.

postgres_set

The `postgres_set` directive is used to set a variable from a single value from the result set. You can specify the row and column to pick the value from. An example configuration is as follows:

```
postgres_set $empname 00 required
```

If you set this directive to `required`, the module will generate a `500 internal server` error if the value to be set is null or out of range.

postgres_escape

The `postgres_escape` directive will escape, quote a value in the `$unquoted` variable, and store the result in the `$escaped` variable, which can be safely used in SQL queries. An example configuration is given as follows:

```
postgres_escape    $user $remote_user;
postgres_escape    $pass $remote_passwd;
```

postgres_connect_timeout

The `postgres_connect_timeout` directive sets a timeout value for connecting to the database.

postgres_result_timeout

The `postgres_result_timeout` directive sets a timeout value for receiving results from the database.

Communicating with MySQL and drizzle (drizzle-nginx)

The `drizzle-nginx` module is an upstream module to communicate with a MySQL or drizzle server. Drizzle is a fork of MySQL, which is optimized for multicore processing and scalability. This module essentially integrates `libdrizzle` into an Nginx module. Like the Nginx PostgreSQL module, this module does not create human-readable text output, but rather a Resty DB format, which is a custom binary format.

You can download the source code for this module from the GitHub repository at `https://github.com/chaoslawful/drizzle-nginx-module`. Please note that you will need to install drizzle and libdrizzle in order to be able to successfully compile this module. You can download drizzle from launchpad at `https://launchpad.net/drizzle`.

This module is useful if you want to directly connect Nginx with a MySQL database. There can be several use-cases of why you would want to do that. You might want to serve pages by directly querying results from a table. You might also want to log things in a database or check certain conditions by querying a database table. Or else, you might want to authenticate a user from an upstream MySQL database. For all such situations and more, this module will be useful.

Explaining directives

The most important directives from the `drizzle-nginx` module are as follows:

drizzle_server

We use the `drizzle_server` directive to specify the drizzle server's name in the form of an IP address or a domain name, and optionally a port. The default port number is `3306`. You can also specify a username and a password. The following options are supported by this directive:

- `user=`: This option defines the database username for login
- `password=`: This option defines the database password, optionally enclosed in quotes, for special characters as shown in the following example configuration:

```
drizzle_server 127.0.0.1:3306 user=user "password=1 2 3"
        dbname=mysql protocol=mysql;
```

- `dbname=`: This option defines the database to be used for the default connection
- `protocol=`: This option defines the target database type, `drizzle`, or `mysql` (the default value is `drizzle`)
- `charset=`: This option is used to explicitly specify the character set for the MySQL connections as shown in the following example configuration:

```
drizzle_server localhost:3306 user=mysqluser password=passwd
                               dbname=mydb charset=utf8;
```

drizzle_keepalive

The `drizzle_keepalive` directive is used to maintain a `keepalive` pool for the target database. The following options are supported by this directive:

- `max=`: This option is set to `0` by default, which means that the `keepalive` connection pooling is disabled. In order to enable it, you must set this value to a value greater than 0.
- `mode=`: The possible values for this parameter are `multi` and `single`. The `single` mode means that the connection pool will not differentiate between multiple `drizzle_server` definitions in the current block, and the pool will apply to all of them, that is, you have one pool for all the `drizzle_server` definitions. In the `multi` mode, the pool will re-use connections that have identical server host names and ports. The default value is `single`.
- `overflow=`: This option specifies what to do when the connection pool is already full while a new database connection is required. Either `reject` or `ignore` can be specified. In case of `reject`, it will reject the current request and return the **503 Service Unavailable** error page. For `ignore`, this module will create a new database connection.

drizzle_query

The `drizzle_query` directive defines the SQL query to be run on the database's backend.

You are allowed to use Nginx variables in place of queries, but you must be careful with SQL injection attacks. You are, therefore, advised to properly sanitize and quote your SQL queries. An example configuration is as follows:

```
location /employees {
    set_unescape_uri $name $arg_name;
    set_quote_sql_str $quoted_name $name;

    drizzle_query "select * from empl where name = $quoted_name";
    drizzle_pass my_backend;
}
```

drizzle_pass

Using the `drizzle_pass` directive, you can pass the current location to another defined MySQL or drizzle-upstream block.

You can use the Nginx variables as values to perform dynamic passing. An example configuration is as follows:

```
upstream backend { localhost:3306 dbname=mydb; }

server {
    location /emp {
        set $srv backend;

        drizzle_query ...;
        drizzle_pass $srv;
    }
}
```

drizzle_connect_timeout

The `drizzle_connect_timeout` directive specifies the timeout value for connecting to the remote server. The value can be an integer with an optional time unit, such as s (second), ms (millisecond), or m (minute). The default time unit is s and the default value is `60 s`.

drizzle_send_query_timeout

The `drizzle_send_query_timeout` directive specifies the timeout value for sending a SQL query to a remote server. The value can be an integer with an optional time unit, such as s (second), ms (millisecond), or m (minute). The default time unit is s and the default value is `60 s`.

drizzle_recv_cols_timeout

The `drizzle_recv_cols_timeout` directive specifies the timeout value for receiving the columns' metadata of the result set to a remote server. The value can be an integer with an optional time unit, such as s (second), ms (millisecond), or m (minute). The default time unit is s and the default value is `60 s`.

drizzle_recv_rows_timeout

The `drizzle_recv_rows_timeout` directive specifies the timeout value for receiving the rows' data of the result set (if any) to a remote server. The value can be an integer with an optional time unit, such as s (second), ms (millisecond), or m (minute). The default time unit is `s` and the default value is `60 s`.

drizzle_buffer_size

The `drizzle_buffer_size` directive specifies the buffer size for server outputs. The default value of this directive depends on the OS page size which would be 4K/8K normally. Larger buffer sizes can result in lower network overheads. However, you have to find the correct value for your workload by experimenting with this number.

drizzle_module_header

The `drizzle_module_header` directive controls whether to output the drizzle header in the response or not. By default, the sending of the header is enabled. This directive can be configured with the following script:

```
X-Resty-DBD-Module: ngx_drizzle 0.1.0
```

Digest Authentication (ngx_http_auth_digest)

In today's world, HTTP basic authentication is too basic and doesn't provide adequate security required by the modern web servers. The reason is that usernames and passwords are sent in clear text unless you use HTTPS. The `ngx_http_auth_digest` module can be used to protect your resources using the HTTP Digest Authentication based on RFC 2617.

The digest authentication module works, and is considered quite stable. However, it is perhaps not tested enough for the real world, so make sure it works in your situation. As this module deals with security, it is always a good idea to test the software thoroughly.

You can download the source code at `https://github.com/samizdatco/nginx-http-auth-digest`.

You can password-protect a directory tree by adding the following code lines into a server section in your Nginx configuration file:

```
auth_digest_user_file /opt/passwd.digest;
location /members{
  auth_digest 'members area; # set the realm for this location block
}
```

Currently, the digest authentication module works with a file generated through the `htdigest` script. The `htdigest` script can be found in your Apache installation or source code. There is also an `htdigest.py` script in this module's source code, which will help you generate a compatible file.

Explaining directives

Some of the most important directives of `ngx_http_auth_digest` are as follows:

auth_digest

The `auth_digest` directive can be defined in the contexts of the server and location. This parameter defines the realm name for authentication. This name should match the name used in creating the `htdigest` file. To selectively disable authentication, set `auth_digest` to `off`. The default value for this directive is `off`.

auth_digest_user_file

The `auth_digest_user_file` directive can be defined in the contexts of the server and location. This directive is used to specify the name of the password file. The password file should be created by the Apache htdigest command (or the included `htdigest.py` script).

auth_digest_timeout

The `auth_digest_timeout` directive can be defined in the contexts of the server and location. This timeout value defines the expiry time of the challenge sent to the client. If the user does not provide the response within this time, the challenge is considered stale, and a new challenge is sent to the client when a resource is requested again or the response comes from the client. The default timeout value is `60 s`.

auth_digest_expires

The `auth_digest_expires` directive can be defined in the contexts of the server and location. This parameter is used to define the expiry time of the nonce value. Once a client successfully authenticates, the nonce value is cached and subsequent requests use the cached value. This parameter defines the duration for which a client can continue to use the nonce value. The default digest expiry value is `10 s`.

auth_digest_replays

The `auth_digest_replays` directive can be defined in the contexts of the server and location. The validity of a cached nonce can also be specified in terms of the number of requests instead of time, by using this directive. Having a high value will increase your shared memory requirements. The default value is 20 replays per nonce.

auth_digest_shm_size

The `auth_digest_shm_size` directive can only be defined in the server's context. This directive specifies the fixed size memory cache used to store information about the active authenticated requests. Once this cache is full, no further authentication will be possible until the active sessions expire. The default size is about 4 MB. The default value allows around 82,000 non-replay requests every 70 seconds.

An example configuration is as follows:

```
auth_digest_user_file /opt/htdigest;
auth_digest_shm_size 4m;    # the storage space allocated for tracking
active sessions

location /restricted {
  auth_digest 'this is a restricted location';
  auth_digest_timeout 60s;
  auth_digest_expires 10s;
  auth_digest_replays 20;
}

location / {
  auth_digest 'restricted';
  location /img {
    auth_digest off; # this location will be accessible  }
}
```

Speeding up web pages (ngx_pagespeed)

The ngx_pagespeed module optimizes the web pages and associated resources to reduce latency and bandwidth. It is capable of rewriting HTML pages and automatically eliminates deficiencies that reduce the performance of your website or web pages. This module is written by Google and is similar to Apache's mod_pagespeed module.

This module reduces the page's load time by automatically applying web performance best practices to pages and associated assets (CSS, JavaScript, and images). It can perform the following types of optimizations:

- Image optimization
- CSS and JavaScript optimization
- Resource inlining
- HTML rewriting
- Cache lifetime extension

In order to enable the module, you have to put pagespeed On in the server or the HTTP block. In addition, you should define the FileCache location and specify which rewrite filters you would like to enable. The following is an example configuration:

```
http {
  pagespeed On;
  pagespeed FileCachePath "/var/cache/ngx_pagespeed/";
  pagespeed EnableFilters combine_css,combine_javascript, add_
instrumentation;
  ...
  ...
}
```

The `FileCachePath` parameter provides the location where rewritten files are cached, and should be a valid path. The `EnableFilters` parameter defines which optimizations will be enabled for the specific location.

Configuring handlers

When the `ngx_pagespeed` module is configured and enabled, a default handler is automatically created, but there are additional handlers in order to monitor the module's activity in more details, which are as follows:

- **Statistics handler**: This handler shows the statistics related to page or resource optimizations, including which pages have been optimized so far, as well as various latency and cache-effectiveness metrics. You can also view the summary of the current configuration that is active at the moment.

- **Messages handler**: If you have enabled and specified a size for the `MessageBufferSize` parameter, this handler will contain a server-wide history of recent logging output from `pagespeed`, including messages that are omitted from the server's logfile based on its log level.

- **Console handler**: This handler shows graphs of issue metrics over time.

- **Beacon handler**: This handler can be used by the `add_instrumentation` filter to report the loading time of pages for your sites, which you can then view via the statistics page.

The following is an example configuration from the module's documentation page:

```
pagespeed on;

# Needs to exist and be writable by nginx.
pagespeed FileCachePath /var/ngx_pagespeed_cache;

# Ensure requests for pagespeed optimized resources go to the
pagespeed handler
# and no extraneous headers get set.
location ~ "\.pagespeed\.([a-z]\.)?[a-z]{2}\.[^.]{10}\.[^.]+" {
  add_header "" "";
```

```
}
location ~ "^/ngx_pagespeed_static/" { }
location ~ "^/ngx_pagespeed_beacon$" { }
location /ngx_pagespeed_statistics { allow 127.0.0.1; deny all; }
# Recent log messages. Like statistics, these are generally not to be
shown to the public, so this has access controls as well.
pagespeed MessageBufferSize 100000;
location /ngx_pagespeed_message { allow 127.0.0.1; deny all; }
```

In order to check if the module is processing your pages or not, you can check the source of a page, which you should be able to see at the X-Page-Speed header through the following code lines:

```
$ curl -I 'http://localhost /index.html/'  |  grep X-Page-Speed
X-Page-Speed: 1.6.29.5-...
```

You can find a complete list of pagespeed filters in the online documentation available at https://developers.google.com/speed/pagespeed/module/using.

Lua scripting (ngx_lua)

If you want the ability to write scripts in your Nginx configuration file, then utilizing the power of Lua by using the ngx_lua module can be a great move. This is a very powerful module with a large number of uses, and provides you with a full programming capability inside the Nginx configuration. It has the following advantages and features:

- This will allow you to perform complicated processing on the incoming request before it's executed, or change the response afterwards

- You can add new headers or remove the existing ones

- You can perform redirects and routing based on complicated program-like logic

- You can create a sophisticated logging framework entirely based on Lua scripts

- You can either block or allow IP addresses

- You can build your own authentication or preprocessing layer on top, without having to write your own C modules and recompiling the Nginx code

Lua is a lightweight, embeddable scripting language, which makes it very suitable for scripting in the configuration file.

This module allows you to run the Lua code during different phases in the Nginx request handling. Before we look at more details of Lua scripting, it is worth looking at the different phases of Nginx request handling.

Each request handled by Nginx goes through the following phases:

Sl. No.	Nginx request-handling phase	Description
1	server selection	A server block is selected based on the request.
2	post read	This phase is executed after a request is read. This allows you to perform actions on the request before it is processed. For example, `HttpRealIpModule` can use this phase to add IP addresses in the request headers.
3	server rewrite	During this phase, URL rewriting can take place. You can select the configuration based on variable values. The `HttpRewrite` module allows you to do so.
4	location selection	During this phase, a location configuration block is selected or matched based on the requested URL.
5	location rewrite	This phase allows you to do rewrites within a selected location-configuration block.
6	preaccess	This phase allows you to carry out certain filters, that is, limit the number of requests per session.
7	access	This phase runs authentications, such as `auth_basic` or `auth_digest`. You can also allow or deny requests based on criteria, such as IP addresses.
8	try files	The core module's `try_files` directive is executed in this phase.
9	content	The actual content generation takes place in this phase. All upstream modules are executed in this phase.
10	log	During this phase, information is logged in the logfiles. Modules such as `access_log` operate within this phase.
11	post action	During this phase, the `post_action` directive of the core module is executed, which allows you to send subrequests to a location or upstream when a request is finished, for example, logging competed requests in a remote MySQL database.

The `nginx_lua` module embeds Lua via the standard Lua interpreter or LuaJIT into Nginx. Please note that you need to install Lua or LuaJIT before you can use this module. This module also has a dependency on another Nginx module called `ngx_devel_kit`. It facilitates the development of new Nginx modules. We will have a detailed look at this module in this chapter as well as in *Chapter 5, Creating Your Own Module*, where we will learn to write our own Nginx module.

Using the Lua API for Nginx, you can communicate with upstream servers in a non-blocking manner in your Lua script. The Lua VM is shared across all the requests handled by a single Nginx worker process to minimize memory usage.

It is possible to use a number of upstream Nginx modules with the `nginx_lua` module. These modules are as follows:

- `lua-resty-memcached`
- `lua-resty-mysql`
- `lua-resty-redis`
- `lua-resty-dns`
- `lua-resty-upload`
- `ngx_memc`
- `ngx_postgres`
- `ngx_redis2`
- `ngx_redis`
- `ngx_proxy`
- `ngx_fastcgi`

An example configuration of the `ngx_lua` module is as follows:

```
    # set search paths for pure Lua external libraries (';;' is the
default path):
    lua_package_path '/home/user/?.lua;/scripts/?.lua;;';

    # set search paths for Lua external libraries written in C (can
also use ';;'):
    lua_package_cpath '/bar/for/?.so;/blah/blah/?.so;;';

    server {
        location /inline_concat {
            # MIME type determined by default_type:
            default_type 'text/plain';
```

```
        set $a "hello";
        set $b "world";
        # inline Lua script
        set_by_lua $res "return ngx.arg[1]..ngx.arg[2]" $a $b;
        echo $res;
    }
```

Explaining directives

Some of the most important directives of ngx_lua are as follows:

lua_package_path

The lua_package_path directive is used to specify the path of the Lua scripts. This value is used by the directives such as set_by_lua and content_by_lua.

You can use the special notation $prefix or ${prefix} in the search path string to indicate the path of the server prefix usually determined by the -p PATH command-line option while starting the Nginx server.

The default value is taken from the LUA_PATH environment variable. If this variable is not defined, then the default search path is used to locate Lua scripts.

set_by_lua or set_by_lua_file

The set_by_lua or set_by_lua_file directives are used to execute a small embedded and blocked Lua script provided as a string. This script can take two parameters as an input and return the result through a return variable. The Nginx event loop is blocked when this code gets executed. You should, therefore, not use this directive to execute long-running codes.

Note that the following API functions are currently disabled within this context. This directive can only write out a value to a single Nginx variable at a time, as shown in the following code snippet:

```
location /testlua {
    set_by_lua $sum '
        local a = 32
        local b = 56
        return a + b;
-- return the $sum value normally
    ';

    echo "sum = $sum
}
```

This directive can be freely mixed with all directives of the `HttpRewriteModule`, `HttpSetMiscModule`, and `HttpArrayVarModule` modules. All these directives will be executed in the same order as they appear in the configuration file. An example configuration is given as follows:

```
set $num 32;
set_by_lua $num2 'tonumber(ngx.var.num) + 1';
```

You can freely use the $ sign inside the Lua scripts provided in this directive as the Nginx variable interpolation is disabled. This directive requires the `ngx_devel_kit` module.

The `set_by_lua_file` directive is similar to the `set_by_lua` directive. The only difference is that the Lua script here is provided in a file. This file can also contain Lua or LuaJIT bytecode instead of a text script.

When a relative path such as `path/file.lua` is given, it will be turned into an absolute path relative to the server prefix path determined by the `-p PATH` command-line option while starting the Nginx server.

By default, the Lua code cache is turned on. This means that the script file is loaded the first time. If you make changes, Nginx configuration will be reloaded. If you are in a development cycle, the code cache can be turned off by using the `lua_code_cache_off` parameter in the configuration file. The following is an example configuration:

```
location /rel_file_concat {
    set $a "foo";
    set $b "bar";
    # script path relative to nginx prefix
    # $ngx_prefix/conf/concat.lua contents:
    #
    #    return ngx.arg[1]..ngx.arg[2]
    #
    set_by_lua_file $res conf/concat.lua $a $b;
    echo $res;
}
```

content_by_lua or content_by_lua_file

The `content_by_lua` or `content_by_lua_file` directives are used to specify a Lua script to execute for every request during the content phase. You can use API calls in this script, and the script is executed in an independent global sandbox.

Since this directive is a content handler, do not use it and the other content handler directives at the same location. For example, this directive and the `proxy_pass` directive should not be used at the same location.

The content_by_lua_file directive is equivalent to content_by_lua, except that in this directive you have to provide the path to a Lua script file instead of writing inline codes. The code in this file is loaded only once if the code cache is turned on, and the relative paths are resolved to absolute paths using the server prefix. An example configuration is shown as follows:

```
location /request_body {
    # force reading request body (default off)
    lua_need_request_body on;
    client_max_body_size 50k;
    client_body_buffer_size 50k;

    content_by_lua 'ngx.print(ngx.var.request_body)';
}
# transparent non-blocking I/O in Lua via subrequests
location /lua {
    # MIME type determined by default_type:
    default_type 'text/plain';

    content_by_lua '
        local res = ngx.location.capture("/some_other_location")
        if res.status == 200 then
            ngx.print(res.body)
        end';
}
```

rewrite_by_lua or rewrite_by_lua_file

The rewrite_by_lua or rewrite_by_lua_file directive executes the Lua code during the rewrite phase. The Lua code can use API calls and is run in a spawned global sandbox.

Note that this handler always runs after the standard HTTP rewrite. So, the following piece of code will not work as expected:

```
location /foo {
    set $a 5; # create and initialize $a
    set $b 13; # create and initialize $b
    rewrite_by_lua 'ngx.var.b = tonumber(ngx.var.a) + 1';
    if ($b = '6') {
        rewrite ^ /bar redirect;
        break;
    }
    echo "res = $b";
}
```

This is because the `if` condition runs before `rewrite_by_lua` even if it is placed after `rewrite_by_lua` in the configuration script.

The correct way of doing this by using Nginx API calls is as follows:

```
location /foo {
    set $a 5; # create and initialize $a
    set $b 13; # create and initialize $b
    rewrite_by_lua '
        ngx.var.b = tonumber(ngx.var.a) + 1
        if tonumber(ngx.var.b) == 6 then
            return ngx.redirect("/bar");
        end
    ';

    echo "res = $b";
}
```

The `rewrite_by_lua` code will always run at the end of the rewrite-request-processing phase unless `rewrite_by_lua_no_postpone` is turned on.

The `rewrite_by_lua_file` directive also runs in the rewrite phase after the standard HTTP rewrite. However, the code is executed from a Lua script file or a bytecode file as shown in the following configuration script:

```
location /script {
        content_by_lua_file /path/to/script/$1.lua;
}
```

access_by_lua or access_by_lua_file

The `access_by_lua` or `access_by_lua_file` directive executes the Lua code during the access phase. This means that the code in this directive will run once per request, and no subrequest will be able to trigger the code.

The Lua code is run after the standard `HttpAccessModule`. Therefore, if you have any blacklisted IPs, they will be denied before this code is executed.

You can use these directives to implement more complex access mechanisms, that is, the ones that communicate with upstream servers, such as a database.

Let us now have a look at a sample ngx_lua configuration to understand the usage of access_by_lua:

```
location / {
        access_by_lua '
```

```
            local ret = ngx.location.capture("/ldap_auth")

            if ret.status == ngx.HTTP_OK then
                return
            end

            if ret.status == ngx.HTTP_FORBIDDEN then
                ngx.exit(ret.status)
            end

            ngx.exit(ngx.HTTP_INTERNAL_SERVER_ERROR)
        ';
    }

    access_by_lua '
            if ngx.var.remote_addr == "10.11.60.220" then
                ngx.exit(ngx.HTTP_FORBIDDEN)
            end ';
```

In the preceding example configuration, the Lua code will run the configuration for a defined location called `ldap_auth`, which will authenticate the user against an LDAP server, and based on a return value, the request either exits with a proper error code (403) or returns normally.

The `access_by_lua` directive allows you to run a Lua script or bytecode using a file. You need to specify the path of the script file in the directive.

Nginx variables can be used in the file to provide flexibility. This, however, carries some risks, and is not ordinarily recommended.

Relative file paths are converted to absolute paths using the server prefix.

It is recommended that you turn on the code cache in the production environment, so that the Lua code is loaded only once. This can provide performance benefits. However, in a development environment, you should not enable the code cache in order to avoid reloading the server every time there is a code change.

The `ngx_lua` module provides complete scripting capabilities while offering very high performance levels. This is especially true if you use the Just In Time (**JIT**) compilation using LuaJIT. This allows you a very wide range of use-cases where this module can be useful.

Reverse IP lookup using the GeoIP module (ngx_http_geoip_module)

The ngx_http_geoip_module does a reverse lookup on the IP of the client using the MaxMind IP database. It resolves the IP address to the place of origin and sets a number for the variables.

This module is not built by default; it should be enabled with the --with-http_ geoip_module configuration parameter. As already mentioned, this module has dependency on the MaxMind GeoIP library.

You need an account with MaxMind and will also need to download several database files that map IP addresses to countries, cities, and even organizations.

One of the key applications, in addition to providing you with more information about the clients, can also be against DDOS attacks. Using the information looked up by this module, you can block or allow traffic coming from countries, cities, regions, and so on. This is a bit crude, but it works. You can use this module as a complement to HttpLimitReqModule and HttpLimitZoneModule. An example configuration is as follows:

```
http {
    geoip_country          countries.dat;
    geoip_city             city.dat;
    geoip_org              org.dat
    geoip_proxy            10.220.136.0/24;
    geoip_proxy            2331:0fb9::/32;
    geoip_proxy_recursive on;
    ...
```

Explaining directives

The following is a list of directives you can use for configuring this module:

geoip_country

The geoip_country directive allows you to specify the name and path of the database file that contains the IP for a country's lookup information. The following variables are available (as well as set by this module) while using this database:

- $geoip_country_code: This is a two-letter country code, for example, DE or US. These codes correspond to ISO 3166-1 alpha-2 standard.

- $geoip_country_code3: This is a three-letter country code, for example, DEU or USA. These codes correspond to ISO 3166-1 alpha-3 standard.

- $geoip_country_name: This gives the complete country name, for example, Russian Federation or United States.

geoip_city

The geoip_city directive allows you to set the name and path of a database file to lookup the city's and region's information based on the client's IP address. The following variables are available and set as well while using this database:

- $geoip_area_code: This gives the telephone area code (US only) associated with the client's IP address. This field in the MaxMind database has been depreciated, so you might not get any information or get outdated information.

- $geoip_city_continent_code: This is a two-letter continent code, for example, EU or AS.

- $geoip_city_country_code: This is a two-letter country code, for example, DE or US. These codes correspond to ISO 3166-1 alpha-2 standard.

- $geoip_city_country_code3: This is a three-letter country code, for example, DEU or USA. These codes correspond to ISO 3166-1 alpha-3 standard.

- $geoip_city_country_name: This gives the country name, for example, Russian Federation or United States.

- $geoip_dma_code: This gives the DMA region code in the US (also known as metro code), which can be found at https://developers.google.com/adwords/api/docs/appendix/cities-DMAregions.

- $geoip_latitude: This gives the latitudinal value of the city.

- $geoip_longitude: This gives the longitudinal value of the city.

- $geoip_region: This is a two-symbol country region code (region, territory, state, province, federal land, and the like), for example, 48 or DC.

- $geoip_region_name: This gives the country's region name (region, territory, state, province, federal land, and the like), for example, Bavaria or District of Columbia.

- $geoip_city: This gives the full city name, for example, Munich or London.

- $geoip_postal_code: This gives the postal code information if available.

geoip_org

The `geoip_org` directive allows you to specify the name and path of the database file to resolve the IP address to an organization. This can be a company name or an institution. Normally, this kind of information is available through the `whois` databases. The following variable is available and set as well while using this option:

- `$geoip_org`: This contains the organization's name, for example, Facebook, Inc.

geoip_proxy

The `geoip_proxy` directive allows you to specify the IP addresses or CIDR of the proxy servers that you "trust". If the client IP address matches this trusted address, the IP address sent in the HTTP header `X-Forwarded-For` is used to do the IP lookup. The `X-Forwarded-For` header is a standard header that is sent by proxy servers to reveal the real IP address of the client. If the proxy server does not choose to do so, it is essentially an anonymizer. The correctness of the IP sent in this header is purely up to the proxy server; therefore, if you trust a specific proxy server to send correct information, you can use this directive to enable lookup on the IP address sent in the `X-Forwarded-For` header.

geoip_proxy_recursive

The `geoip_proxy_recursive` directive allows you to enable recursive IP lookup. If recursive lookup is enabled, the last untrusted address sent in the `X-Forwarded-For` header will be used for the IP lookup.

If Nginx is working behind a proxy, you can also use `HttpRealIpModule`. This module allows you to change the client's IP address to a value from the request header (for example, `X-Real-IP` or `X-Forwarded-For`).

Doing healthchecks

Here we will learn about various modules to keep a track of the healthy upstreams.

ngx_http_healthcheck_module

If your Nginx server works with a lot of upstream servers for providing various services and content, keeping track of which upstream servers are still healthy and working is very important, especially if they are third-party or external servers. This module allows you to keep track of healthy backends.

This is how it works. When an upstream server responds with a 200+ status code, and the response optionally comes back with a body, it is marked as good; otherwise, it is marked as bad. This module also has an HTTP healthcheck page where you can see the current status of the backends. This is quite similar to the `haproxy` or `varnish` healthchecks.

This module inserts a healthcheck event into Nginx's event tree. When that triggers, it starts a peer connection with the backend and sends as well as receives data. When the heathcheck is over or gets timed out, it updates the health of the backend in a shared memory area. The following is an example configuration:

```
http {

  upstream check_upstreams {
    server server1.com;
    server server2.com;
    healthcheck_enabled;
    healthcheck_delay 1000;
    healthcheck_timeout 1000;
    healthcheck_failcount 1;
    healthcheck_expected 'BACKEND_ALIVE';
    healthcheck_send "GET /health HTTP/1.0" 'Host: www.websitename.
com';
  }
  ...
  location /health_status {
      healthcheck_status;
  }
  ...
}
```

Explaining directives

Some of the most important directives of the `ngx_http_healthcheck_module` are as follows:

healthcheck_enabled

The `healthcheck_enabled` module's context is upstream and enables health checking on the upstream servers defined in the specific upstream block. This, in the preceding example, would be `server1` and `server2`.

healthcheck_delay

For each upstream server, the `healthcheck_delay` directive defines the delay between two healthchecks. The default value is `1000 ms`.

healthcheck_timeout

The `healthcheck_timeout` directive defines the timeout value for the healthcheck operation. If the healthcheck operation is taking too long because the backend is slow in responding, the process will stop after the timeout has elapsed. The default value is `2000 ms`.

healthcheck_failcount

The `healthcheck_failcount` directive gives the number of good or bad healthchecks in a row it takes to switch the current health status (good to bad or bad to good). The default value is `2`.

healthcheck_send

The `healthcheck_send` directive is a required directive that allows you to decide what to send to do a healthcheck. This can be a simple HTTP GET command or something more complex. Each argument is appended by `\r\n` and the entire block is suffixed with another `\r\n`. The following is an example configuration:

```
healthcheck_send 'GET /health HTTP/1.0'
  'Host: www.yourhost.com';
```

Note that you probably want to end your healthcheck with some directive that closes the connection, for example, `Connection: close`.

healthcheck_expected

The `healthcheck_expected` directive allows you to specify what to expect in return from the upstream server as a response to mark it as healthy. Any other response or no response will mark the host as down. This refers to the response in the HTTP body and not the headers. If this directive is missing, a simple response code of 200 will be enough.

healthcheck_buffer

The `healthcheck_buffer` directive gives the size of the buffer where the response from the backend will be temporarily stored for checking. Make sure you allocate enough memory not only for the body but also for the headers that you expect to receive back in response.

Load balancing

There are a number of third-party Nginx modules available, which allow you to distribute load among upstream servers based on a hashing mechanism or on a least-busy basis. There are various hashing mechanisms available for load balancing, some of which are available via third-party modules. Here, we will just take a brief look at some of the options available to you.

Consistent hashing

The `ngx_http_upstream_consistent_hash` module allows you to load balance using a consistent hash ring. Consistent hashing is a special hashing algorithm that is quite good when you have to rehash frequently because a new machine or server is added or removed from the pool.

This module is compatible with the `php-memcached` module, and you can store values in the `memcached` cluster that this module can read from. You can find more details about this module at `http://wiki.nginx.org/HttpUpstreamConsistentHash`.

There is another similar module that uses the Ketama consistent hashing library to compute a hash on a configuration variable, that is, Request URI. Check out more information about this at `http://wiki.nginx.org/HttpUpstreamKetamaCHashModule`.

Least busy

The `ngx_http_upstream_fair_module` module allows you to do load balancing based on which upstream is least busy.

This module also provides a status page where you can view the current status of load balancing.

This module uses **Weighted Least-Connection Round Robin (WLC-RR)** with a number of possible variations. More information on this module is available at `http://wiki.nginx.org/HttpUpstreamFairModule`.

Configuration variable hashing

Configuration variable hashing is probably the most random hashing you can do. You can choose to do a hash on one of the available variables, that is, `$request_uri` or HTTP headers or a combination of both. This module uses CRC-32 to compute the hash on a specified variable.

More information on this is available at `http://wiki.nginx.org/HttpUpstreamRequestHashModule`.

Summary

In this chapter, we looked at various useful third-party Nginx modules that are not distributed with the source code by default. There are many more useful modules available that you can find on GitHub. Please do pay attention to the fact that the module is stable enough to be used in the production environment. Always do some testing first and then carefully move the modules in the production environments. The Nginx community will take no responsibility for any problems that you may encounter as a result of using these modules.

In the next chapter, we will discuss developing our own Nginx module, which will be the first step into the world of custom module development.

5
Creating Your Own Module

Nginx allows you to extend functionality by writing new modules in plain C. This chapter gives a brief introduction to creating your own modules. It is a quick reference to the module system in Nginx, and the internal architecture of Nginx, which makes extension possible. It introduces different categories of modules and add-ons you can create at a high level. This chapter will also contain a quick introduction of NDK, a special module in Nginx used as a basis of other modules.

The topics covered are as follows:

- Concept of module chaining and delegation in Nginx
- Handler modules
- Filter modules
- Load balancer modules
- **Nginx Development Toolkit (NDK)**: The NDK is an Nginx module that is designed to extend the core functionality of the excellent Nginx web server, in a way that can be used as a basis of other Nginx modules
- Sample source code of a custom Nginx module

At the end of this chapter, the advanced users will have an idea about internal Nginx architecture, and what is the basis of creating your own third-party module. Readers should be able to know how to use NDK; the source code will help them see a very simple self-written module in action.

Nginx module delegation

Nginx has a very modular architecture. All major operations that Nginx performs are carried out by modules. All Nginx modules are built in at compile time and are not loaded dynamically.

Module delegation can also be called **module chaining**. The core pretty much does the basic stuff related to setting up the connection and taking care of things related to the protocol. It then sets up a chain of modules to execute, each taking care of a certain phase or stage of request processing.

The module-based noncentralized architecture makes it possible for advanced users to develop a module that does something they want.

The following are the different types of Nginx modules.

Handlers

There is a handler for each defined location in the configuration file. When the server starts up, handlers are attached or bound to a location. Ideally there should only be one handler to a location; if there are more than one defined in the configuration file, only one of them will be valid (typically the last one). Handlers end in the following three ways: successfully when all is good, fail when there is an error, or they will not process the request and will let the default handler process it.

Load balancers

The load balancer or upstream module forwards your requests to one of the many configured backends or upstreams. Nginx, by default, has two load-balancing modules built in: **Round Robin** and the **IP Hash** method (look at `ngx_http_upstream_module`). There are other third-party modules available that allow you to do load balancing based on various hashing mechanisms, for example, Consistent Hashing.

Filters

After a handler produces a response, the filters are executed. Filters do the postprocessing on the handler's response. One example can be that you need to compress the response, or add certain headers to it. Multiple filters can associate with each location.

Order of execution

The order of execution of Nginx filters is determined when they are compiled. You can see the order of the execution after compiling the code in `ngx_modules.c`. This file is generated on the fly by the `modules` script, which is found at `nginx/auto/`. This script makes sure that it maintains the correct order of the module and filter execution.

The built-in modules do need a specific order, for example, a gzip filter should run after the header and body filters have been executed. The new custom modules are generally executed in the end.

Filters do not execute in a fully blocked manner, rather the output of the filters is streamed through the chain of filters. By default, one filter processes some data and passes it on to the next module and so on. The amount of data processed at a time is usually a multiple of the page size. Different modules, for example, gzip, allow you to adjust this value.

The extended "Hello world" module

Now we will proceed towards creating a simple Nginx module. This module will print a configurable text in your browser whenever you enter a specific location. This is a very simple module and the idea is to just introduce the core concepts of how to create an Nginx module. This is based on and is an enhanced version of the simple Hello world module found at `http://blog.zhuzhaoyuan.com/2009/08/creating-a-hello-world-nginx-module/`. This module is an example of a handler module.

Writing and compiling a module

The first thing you have to do is to obviously create a folder for your new module. Create it anywhere other than the Nginx source tree. You should create the following two files to start with:

- `config`
- `ngx_http_hello_module.c`

The contents of the `config` file will depend on what kind of module you are writing.

For this simple module, it will look like the following code:

```
ngx_addon_name=ngx_http_hello_module
HTTP_MODULES="$HTTP_MODULES ngx_http_hello_module"
NGX_ADDON_SRCS="$NGX_ADDON_SRCS $ngx_addon_dir/ngx_http_hello_
module.c"
```

The file is quite self-explanatory. In the second line we are adding the module to a list of HTTP modules. Depending on which module type you are writing, you will need to add it to a different list. You can see the full list in the `modules` script found at `nginx/auto/`.

Before compiling, the module needs to be explicitly specified using the `configure` script as in the following code. The `add-module` list should contain a list of all third-party modules you want to include in the compilation.

```
./configure --add-module=path/to/your/new/module/directory
```

This has to be followed by `make` and `make install` as usual.

The "Hello world" source code

The following code is from `ngx_http_hello_module.c`:

```c
#include <ngx_config.h>
#include <ngx_core.h>
#include <ngx_http.h>


static char *ngx_http_hello(ngx_conf_t *cf, void *post, void
  *data);

static ngx_conf_post_handler_pt ngx_http_hello_p = ngx_http_hello;

/*
 * The structure will hold the value of the
 * module directive hello
 */
typedef struct {
  ngx_str_t    name;
} ngx_http_hello_loc_conf_t;

/* The function which initializes memory for the module configuration
structure
 */
static void *
ngx_http_hello_create_loc_conf(ngx_conf_t *cf)
{
  ngx_http_hello_loc_conf_t  *conf;

  conf = ngx_pcalloc(cf->pool, sizeof(ngx_http_hello_loc_conf_t));
  if (conf == NULL) {
    return NULL;
  }

  return conf;
}
```

```
/*
 * The command array or array, which holds one subarray for each
module
 * directive along with a function which validates the value of the
 * directive and also initializes the main handler of this module
 */
static ngx_command_t ngx_http_hello_commands[] = {
  { ngx_string("hello"),
    NGX_HTTP_LOC_CONF|NGX_CONF_TAKE1,
    ngx_conf_set_str_slot,
    NGX_HTTP_LOC_CONF_OFFSET,
    offsetof(ngx_http_hello_loc_conf_t, name),
    &ngx_http_hello_p },

  ngx_null_command
};


static ngx_str_t hello_string;

/*
 * The module context has hooks , here we have a hook for creating
 * location configuration
 */
static ngx_http_module_t ngx_http_hello_module_ctx = {
  NULL,                         /* preconfiguration */
  NULL,                         /* postconfiguration */

  NULL,                         /* create main configuration */
  NULL,                         /* init main configuration */

  NULL,                         /* create server configuration */
  NULL,                         /* merge server configuration */

  ngx_http_hello_create_loc_conf, /* create location configuration */
  NULL                          /* merge location configuration */
};


/*
 * The module which binds the context and commands
 *
 */
ngx_module_t ngx_http_hello_module = {
  NGX_MODULE_V1,
```

```
        &ngx_http_hello_module_ctx,     /* module context */
        ngx_http_hello_commands,        /* module directives */
        NGX_HTTP_MODULE,                /* module type */
        NULL,                           /* init master */
        NULL,                           /* init module */
        NULL,                           /* init process */
        NULL,                           /* init thread */
        NULL,                           /* exit thread */
        NULL,                           /* exit process */
        NULL,                           /* exit master */
        NGX_MODULE_V1_PADDING
    };

    /*
     * Main handler function of the module.
     */
    static ngx_int_t
    ngx_http_hello_handler(ngx_http_request_t *r)
    {
        ngx_int_t      rc;
        ngx_buf_t      *b;
        ngx_chain_t    out;

        /* we response to 'GET' and 'HEAD' requests only */
        if (!(r->method & (NGX_HTTP_GET|NGX_HTTP_HEAD))) {
            return NGX_HTTP_NOT_ALLOWED;
        }

        /* discard request body, since we don't need it here */
        rc = ngx_http_discard_request_body(r);

        if (rc != NGX_OK) {
            return rc;
        }

        /* set the 'Content-type' header */
        r->headers_out.content_type_len = sizeof("text/html") - 1;
        r->headers_out.content_type.len = sizeof("text/html") - 1;
        r->headers_out.content_type.data = (u_char *) "text/html";

        /* send the header only, if the request type is http 'HEAD' */
        if (r->method == NGX_HTTP_HEAD) {
            r->headers_out.status = NGX_HTTP_OK;
            r->headers_out.content_length_n = hello_string.len;
```

```
    return ngx_http_send_header(r);
}

/* allocate a buffer for your response body */
b = ngx_pcalloc(r->pool, sizeof(ngx_buf_t));
if (b == NULL) {
  return NGX_HTTP_INTERNAL_SERVER_ERROR;
}

/* attach this buffer to the buffer chain */
out.buf = b;
out.next = NULL;

/* adjust the pointers of the buffer */
b->pos = hello_string.data;
b->last = hello_string.data + hello_string.len;
b->memory = 1;    /* this buffer is in memory */
b->last_buf = 1;  /* this is the last buffer in the buffer chain
  */

/* set the status line */
r->headers_out.status = NGX_HTTP_OK;
r->headers_out.content_length_n = hello_string.len;

/* send the headers of your response */
rc = ngx_http_send_header(r);

if (rc == NGX_ERROR || rc > NGX_OK || r->header_only) {
  return rc;
}

/* send the buffer chain of your response */
return ngx_http_output_filter(r, &out);
}

/*
 * Function for the directive hello , it validates its value
 * and copies it to a static variable to be printed later
 */
static char *
ngx_http_hello(ngx_conf_t *cf, void *post, void *data)
{
  ngx_http_core_loc_conf_t *clcf;
```

```
clcf = ngx_http_conf_get_module_loc_conf(cf,
  ngx_http_core_module);
clcf->handler = ngx_http_hello_handler;

ngx_str_t  *name = data; // i.e., first field of
  ngx_http_hello_loc_conf_t

if (ngx_strcmp(name->data, "") == 0) {
  return NGX_CONF_ERROR;
}
hello_string.data = name->data;
hello_string.len = ngx_strlen(hello_string.data);

return NGX_CONF_OK;
}
```

A sample configuration for this extended `hello world` module could look as follows:

```
server {
listen 8080;
server_name localhost;

location / {
hello 'Hello World';
  }
}
```

Components of the Nginx module

There are many components on an Nginx module depending on the type of the module. We will now discuss those parts that are common to almost all the modules. The intention is to present to you a reference in an easy to understand way so that you can be ready to write your own module.

Module configuration structures

Modules can define one configuration for each of the configuration file's configuration contexts—there is an individual structure for the main, server, and location contexts. It is OK for most modules to simply have a location structure. These structures should be named as `convention  ngx_http_<module name>_(main|srv|loc)_conf_t`. The following is the code snippet from the sample module:

```
typedef struct {
  ngx_str_t    name;
} ngx_http_hello_loc_conf_t;
```

The members of this structure should use Nginx's special data types (ngx_uint_t, ngx_flag_t, and ngx_str_t), which are simply aliases for basic/primitive types. You can look into core/nginx_config.h in the source tree for the data type definitions.

There should be as many members of this structure as the module directives. In the preceding example our module only has one directive, so we can already tell that this module will support a single directive/option at the location level, which will populate the member name of this structure.

As it must be obvious by now, that the elements in the configuration structure are filled by module directives defined in the configuration file.

Module directives

After you have defined the place where the value of the module directives will be stored, it is time to define the name of the module directives and what kind and type of arguments they will accept. A module's directives are defined in a static array of the ngx_command_t type structure. Looking at the example code we previously wrote, the following is what the directives structure looks like:

```
static ngx_command_t ngx_http_hello_commands[] = {
  { ngx_string("hello"),
  NGX_HTTP_LOC_CONF|NGX_CONF_TAKE1,
  ngx_conf_set_str_slot,
  NGX_HTTP_LOC_CONF_OFFSET,
  offsetof(ngx_http_hello_loc_conf_t, name),
  &ngx_http_hello_p },

  ngx_null_command
};
```

The preceding structure may look a little bit complicated. However, we will now look at each one of those to understand them a little better.

The first argument defines the name of the directive. This is of type ngx_str and is instantiated with the directive name, for example, ngx_str("hello"). An ngx_str_t data type is a struct type with data and length elements. Nginx uses this data structure for all the strings.

The second argument defines the type of the directive, and what kind of arguments it accepts. The acceptable values for these parameters should be bitwise ordered with each other. The possibilities are as follows:

```
NGX_HTTP_MAIN_CONF: directive should be used in main section
NGX_HTTP_SRV_CONF : directive should be used in the server section
NGX_HTTP_LOC_CONF : directive should be used in the location
    section
NGX_HTTP_UPS_CONF : directive should be used in the upstream
    section
NGX_CONF_NOARGS    : directive will take no arguments
NGX_CONF_TAKE1     : directive will take 1 argument
NGX_CONF_TAKE2     : directive will take 2 arguments
...
NGX_CONF_TAKE7     : directive will take 7 arguments
NGX_CONF_TAKE12    : directive will take 1 or 2 arguments
NGX_CONF_TAKE13    : directive will take 1 or 3 arguments
NGX_CONF_TAKE23    : directive will take 2 or 3 arguments
NGX_CONF_TAKE123   : directive will take 1, 2 or 3 arguments
NGX_CONF_TAKE1234 : directive will take 1, 2 , 3 or 4 arguments

NGX_CONF_FLAG      : directive accepts a boolean value from "on" or
    "off"
NGX_CONF_1MORE     : directive requires at least one argument
NGX_CONF_2MORE     : directive requires at least at least two
    arguments
```

Please see the full details in `ngx_conf_file.h` found in the `core` folder.

The maximum number of arguments that a directive can take is eight (0-7) as defined in `core/ngx_conf_file.h`, as shown in the following code:

```
#define NGX_CONF_MAX_ARGS    8
```

In the preceding example, we only use a single element in the array, as we are providing values for a single `ngx_command_t` structure.

The third argument is a function pointer. This is a setup function that takes the value provided for the directive in the configuration file and stores it in the appropriate element of the structure. This function can take the following three arguments:

- Pointer to `ngx_conf_t` (`main`, `srv`, or `loc`) structure, which contains the values of the directive in the configuration file
- Pointer to the target `ngx_command_t` structure where the value will be stored
- Pointer to the module's custom configuration structure (can be NULL)

Nginx provides a number of functions that can be used to set the values for the built-in data types. These functions include:

- `ngx_conf_set_flag_slot`
- `ngx_conf_set_str_slot`
- `ngx_conf_set_str_array_slot`
- `ngx_conf_set_keyval_slot`
- `ngx_conf_set_num_slot`
- `ngx_conf_set_size_slot`
- `ngx_conf_set_off_slot`
- `ngx_conf_set_msec_slot`
- `ngx_conf_set_sec_slot`
- `ngx_conf_set_bufs_slot`
- `ngx_conf_set_enum_slot`
- `ngx_conf_set_bitmask_slot`

Some of these are described as follows:

- `ngx_conf_set_flag_slot`: This translates on or off to 1 or 0
- `ngx_conf_set_str_slot`: This saves a string as `ngx_str_t`
- `ngx_conf_set_num_slot`: This parses a number and saves it to an integer
- `ngx_conf_set_size_slot`: This parses a data size (5k, 2m, and so on) and saves it to `size_t`

Module authors can also pass the pointer to their own function here, if the built-in functions are not sufficient for their purpose, for example, if the string needs to be interpreted in a certain way instead of just being stored as it is.

In order to specify where these built-in (or custom) functions will store the directive values, you have to specify `conf` and `offset` as the next two arguments. `conf` specifies the type of the structure where the value will be stored (`main`, `srv`, `loc`) and `offset` specifies which part of this configuration structure to store it in. The following is the `offset` of the element in the structure, that is, `offsetof(ngx_http_hello_loc_conf_t, name)`.

The last element is often NULL, and at the moment we can choose to ignore it.

The last element of the command array is `ngx_null_command`, which indicates the termination.

The module context

The third structure in an Nginx module that needs to be defined is a static `ngx_http_module_t` structure, which just has the function pointers for creating the `main`, `srv`, and `loc` configurations, and merging them together. Its name is `ngx_http_<module name>_module_ctx`. The function references that you can provide are as follows:

- Pre configuration
- Post configuration
- Creating the main `conf`
- Initializing the main `conf`
- Creating the server `conf`
- Merging it with the main `conf`
- Creating the location `conf`
- Merging it with the server `conf`

These take different arguments depending on what they're doing. The following is the structure definition, taken from `http/ngx_http_config.h`, so you can see the different function signatures of the callbacks:

```
typedef struct {
    ngx_int_t    (*preconfiguration)(ngx_conf_t *cf);
    ngx_int_t    (*postconfiguration)(ngx_conf_t *cf);

    void         *(*create_main_conf)(ngx_conf_t *cf);
    char         *(*init_main_conf)(ngx_conf_t *cf, void *conf);

    void         *(*create_srv_conf)(ngx_conf_t *cf);
    char         *(*merge_srv_conf)(ngx_conf_t *cf, void *prev, void
      *conf);

    void         *(*create_loc_conf)(ngx_conf_t *cf);
    char         *(*merge_loc_conf)(ngx_conf_t *cf, void *prev, void
      *conf);
} ngx_http_module_t;
```

You can set functions you don't need to NULL, and Nginx will accept it, and do the right thing.

The create functions such as create main `conf`, create server `conf`, and create location `conf` normally just allocate memory for the structures (such as `malloc()`) and initialize the elements as default values. The functions such as initialize main `conf`, and merge with main `conf` provide the opportunity to override the default values.

During merging, the module authors can look for duplicate definitions of elements and throw errors if there is a problem with directives provided by configuration authors in the configuration file.

Most module authors just use the last two elements as such: a function to allocate memory for `ngx_loc_conf` (`main`, `srv`, or `loc`) configuration, and a function to set defaults and merge this configuration into a merged location configuration (called `ngx_http_<module name >_merge_loc_conf`).

The following is an example module context structure:

```
/*
 * The module context has hooks , here we have a hook for creating
 * location configuration
 */
static ngx_http_module_t ngx_http_hello_module_ctx = {
  NULL,                          /* preconfiguration */
  NULL,                          /* postconfiguration */
  NULL,                          /* create main configuration */
  NULL,                          /* init main configuration */
  NULL,                          /* create server configuration */
  NULL,                          /* merge server configuration */
  ngx_http_hello_create_loc_conf, /* create location configuration
  */
  NULL                           /* merge location configuration
  */
};
```

We can have a closer look now at these functions, which set up the location based on configuration.

create_loc_conf

The following is what a basic `create_loc_conf` function looks like. It takes a directive structure (`ngx_conf_t`) and returns a module configuration structure that is newly allocated.

```
/* The function which initializes memory for the module configuration
structure
 */
static void *
ngx_http_hello_create_loc_conf(ngx_conf_t *cf)
{
  ngx_http_hello_loc_conf_t  *conf;

  conf = ngx_pcalloc(cf->pool, sizeof(ngx_http_hello_loc_conf_t));
  if (conf == NULL) {
```

```
        return NULL;
    }

    return conf;
}
```

The Nginx memory allocation takes care of freeing the memory if you use the built-ins ngx_palloc (a malloc wrapper) or ngx_pcalloc (a calloc wrapper).

merge_loc_conf

The sample module we created does not contain a merge location conf function. However, we can look at the following sample code just to explain some basic concepts. You generally need a merge function if a directive can be defined multiple times. It is your job to define a merge function that can set the appropriate value in case it is defined multiple times or in multiple locations.

```
static char *
   ngx_http_example_merge_loc_conf(ngx_conf_t *cf, void *parent,
   void *child)
{
   ngx_http_example_loc_conf_t *prev = parent;
   ngx_http_example_loc_conf_t *conf = child;

   ngx_conf_merge_uint_value(conf->val1, prev->val1, 10);
   ngx_conf_merge_uint_value(conf->val2, prev->val2, 20);

   if (conf->val1 < 1) {
     ngx_conf_log_error(NGX_LOG_EMERG, cf, 0,
       "value 1 must be equal or more than 1");
     return NGX_CONF_ERROR;
   }
   if (conf->val2 < conf->val1) {
     ngx_conf_log_error(NGX_LOG_EMERG, cf, 0,
        "val2 must be equal or more than val1");
     return NGX_CONF_ERROR;
   }

   return NGX_CONF_OK;
}
```

Nginx provides very useful merging built-in functions for various data types (ngx_conf_merge_<data type>_value). These functions take the arguments as follows:

- The location's value (can refer to an element in a structure)
- The value to use if the first value is not set
- The default value if both first and second values are not set

The first argument stores the result. See `core/ngx_conf_file.h` for a full list of available merge functions. The following is an extract from the file:

```
#define ngx_conf_merge_value(conf, prev, default) \
  if (conf == NGX_CONF_UNSET) { \
  conf = (prev == NGX_CONF_UNSET) ? default : prev; \
  }

#define ngx_conf_merge_ptr_value(conf, prev, default) \
  if (conf == NGX_CONF_UNSET_PTR) { \
    conf = (prev == NGX_CONF_UNSET_PTR) ? default : prev; \
  }

#define ngx_conf_merge_uint_value(conf, prev, default) \
  if (conf == NGX_CONF_UNSET_UINT) { \
    conf = (prev == NGX_CONF_UNSET_UINT) ? default : prev; \
  }

#define ngx_conf_merge_msec_value(conf, prev, default) \
  if (conf == NGX_CONF_UNSET_MSEC) { \
    conf = (prev == NGX_CONF_UNSET_MSEC) ? default : prev; \
  }

#define ngx_conf_merge_sec_value(conf, prev, default) \
  if (conf == NGX_CONF_UNSET) { \
    conf = (prev == NGX_CONF_UNSET) ? default : prev; \
  }

#define ngx_conf_merge_size_value(conf, prev, default) \
  if (conf == NGX_CONF_UNSET_SIZE) { \
    conf = (prev == NGX_CONF_UNSET_SIZE) ? default : prev; \
  }

#define ngx_conf_merge_off_value(conf, prev, default) \
  if (conf == NGX_CONF_UNSET) { \
    conf = (prev == NGX_CONF_UNSET) ? default : prev; \
  }

#define ngx_conf_merge_str_value(conf, prev, default) \
  if (conf.data == NULL) { \
  if (prev.data) { \
    conf.len = prev.len; \
     conf.data = prev.data; \
    } else { \
    conf.len = sizeof(default) - 1; \
    conf.data = (u_char *) default; \
    } \
  }

#define ngx_conf_merge_bufs_value(conf, prev, default_num,
```

```
    default_size)          \
    if (conf.num == 0) { \
      if (prev.num) { \
        conf.num = prev.num; \
        conf.size = prev.size; \
        } else { \
        conf.num = default_num; \
        conf.size = default_size; \
        } \
}
```

As you can see these functions are defined as macros, and they are expanded and placed inline in the code during compilation.

Another thing to learn is how to log errors. The function outputs to the log file using the `ngx_conf_log_error` function—where you specify a log level—and returns `NGX_CONF_ERROR`, which stops server startup.

There are several log levels defined in Nginx. These are defined in `ngx_log.h`. The following is an extract from the code:

```
#define NGX_LOG_STDERR          0
#define NGX_LOG_EMERG           1
#define NGX_LOG_ALERT           2
#define NGX_LOG_CRIT            3
#define NGX_LOG_ERR             4
#define NGX_LOG_WARN            5
#define NGX_LOG_NOTICE          6
#define NGX_LOG_INFO            7
#define NGX_LOG_DEBUG           8
```

The module definition

The next structure a new module should define is the module definition structure or the `ngx_module_t` structure. The variable is called `ngx_http_<module name>_module`. This structure binds together the structures we have been defining until now. You have to provide the pointers to the context and directives structures, as well as the remaining callbacks (exit thread, exit process, and so on). The module definition can act like a key to look up data associated with a particular module. The module definition of our custom module looks as follows:

```
#define NGX_MODULE_V1           0, 0, 0, 0, 0, 0, 1
#define NGX_MODULE_V1_PADDING   0, 0, 0, 0, 0, 0, 0, 0
struct ngx_module_s {
  ngx_uint_t            ctx_index;
  ngx_uint_t            index;
  ngx_uint_t            spare0;
```

```
ngx_uint_t              spare1;
ngx_uint_t              spare2;
ngx_uint_t              spare3;
ngx_uint_t              version;
void                    *ctx;
ngx_command_t           *commands;
ngx_uint_t              type;
ngx_int_t               (*init_master)(ngx_log_t *log);
ngx_int_t               (*init_module)(ngx_cycle_t *cycle);
ngx_int_t               (*init_process)(ngx_cycle_t *cycle);
ngx_int_t               (*init_thread)(ngx_cycle_t *cycle);
void                    (*exit_thread)(ngx_cycle_t *cycle);
void                    (*exit_process)(ngx_cycle_t *cycle);
void                    (*exit_master)(ngx_cycle_t *cycle);
uintptr_t               spare_hook0;
uintptr_t               spare_hook1;
uintptr_t               spare_hook2;
uintptr_t               spare_hook3;
uintptr_t               spare_hook4;
uintptr_t               spare_hook5;
uintptr_t               spare_hook6;
uintptr_t               spare_hook7;
};
```

You can see that the macros `NGX_MODULE_V1` and `NGX_MODULE_V1_PADDING` provide the values for the structure elements before and after the highlighted section in the preceding code. This is a detail we don't need to get into at the moment. For now, look at the following example on how to use them:

```
/*
 * The module which binds the context and commands
 *
 */
ngx_module_t ngx_http_hello_module = {
  NGX_MODULE_V1,
  &ngx_http_hello_module_ctx,      /* module context */
  ngx_http_hello_commands,         /* module directives */
  NGX_HTTP_MODULE,                 /* module type */
  NULL,                            /* init master */
  NULL,                            /* init module */
  NULL,                            /* init process */
  NULL,                            /* init thread */
  NULL,                            /* exit thread */
  NULL,                            /* exit process */
  NULL,                            /* exit master */
  NGX_MODULE_V1_PADDING
};
```

You can see from the comments in the preceding code what each argument means. The first and last elements are the masks that hide the additional structure elements mainly because we don't need them, and they are place holders for the future. We also provide a module type, which in this case is HTTP. Most of the user-defined custom modules will be of this type. You can define other types such as CORE, MAIL, EVENT and so on; however, they are mostly not used as add-on module types.

The handler function

The final piece of the puzzle after all the preparation work and configuration structures is the actual handler function which does all the work. The handler function for our sample module is as follows:

```
/*
 * Main handler function of the module.
 */
static ngx_int_t
  ngx_http_hello_handler(ngx_http_request_t *r)
{
  ngx_int_t    rc;
  ngx_buf_t    *b;
  ngx_chain_t  out;

  /* we response to 'GET' and 'HEAD' requests only */
  if (!(r->method & (NGX_HTTP_GET|NGX_HTTP_HEAD))) {
    return NGX_HTTP_NOT_ALLOWED;
  }

  /* discard request body, since we don't need it here */
  rc = ngx_http_discard_request_body(r);

  if (rc != NGX_OK) {
    return rc;
  }

  /* set the 'Content-type' header */
  r->headers_out.content_type_len = sizeof("text/html") - 1;
  r->headers_out.content_type.data = (u_char *) "text/html";
  /* send the header only, if the request type is http 'HEAD' */
  if (r->method == NGX_HTTP_HEAD) {
    r->headers_out.status = NGX_HTTP_OK;
    r->headers_out.content_length_n = hello_string.len;

  return ngx_http_send_header(r);
  }

  /* allocate a buffer for your response body */
  b = ngx_pcalloc(r->pool, sizeof(ngx_buf_t));
```

```
    if (b == NULL) {
      return NGX_HTTP_INTERNAL_SERVER_ERROR;
    }

    /* attach this buffer to the buffer chain */
    out.buf = b;
    out.next = NULL;

    /* adjust the pointers of the buffer */
    b->pos = hello_string.data;
    b->last = hello_string.data + hello_string.len;
    b->memory = 1;     /* this buffer is in memory */
    b->last_buf = 1;   /* this is the last buffer in the buffer chain
      */

    /* set the status line */
    r->headers_out.status = NGX_HTTP_OK;
    r->headers_out.content_length_n = hello_string.len;

    /* send the headers of your response */
    rc = ngx_http_send_header(r);

    if (rc == NGX_ERROR || rc > NGX_OK || r->header_only) {
      return rc;
    }

    /* send the buffer chain of your response */
    return ngx_http_output_filter(r, &out);
}
```

There are a few things to learn in the code. As explained earlier, this module basically prints whatever you had provided in the configuration. For example, according to the following configuration, this module will make sure that it prints **Hello World** whenever you open http://localhost:8080:

```
server {
listen 8080;
server_name localhost;

location / {
hello 'Hello World';
  }
}
```

This method receives the HTTP request as an argument. If your module only responds to a certain type of HTTP requests, you can check by looking at the HTTP request structure. For example, our module only responds to HTTP GET and HEAD requests as checked by this chunk of code; otherwise it returns "error code 405 (not allowed)".

All the HTTP error codes are defined in ngx_http_request.h as follows:

```
/* we response to 'GET' and 'HEAD' requests only */
if (!(r->method & (NGX_HTTP_GET|NGX_HTTP_HEAD))) {
  return NGX_HTTP_NOT_ALLOWED;
}
```

Next, we discard the request body as in this module we don't need it. In several modules, one will write a body that will be important, however, right now we don't care about it. By discarding the request body, Nginx will not read the request body fully for processing and will not allocate memory for it internally.

Next we set some HTTP headers in our response. All headers you can set in the response can be accessed through the headers_out member of the HTTP request structure. The headers_out structure allows you to set a number of outgoing headers. The extract from ngx_http_request.h is as follows:

```
typedef struct {
  ngx_list_t                          headers;

  ngx_uint_t                          status;
  ngx_str_t                           status_line;

  ngx_table_elt_t                     *server;
  ngx_table_elt_t                     *date;
  ngx_table_elt_t                     *content_length;
  ngx_table_elt_t                     *content_encoding;
  ngx_table_elt_t                     *location;
  ngx_table_elt_t                     *refresh;
  ngx_table_elt_t                     *last_modified;
  ngx_table_elt_t                     *content_range;
  ngx_table_elt_t                     *accept_ranges;
  ngx_table_elt_t                     *www_authenticate;
  ngx_table_elt_t                     *expires;
  ngx_table_elt_t                     *etag;

  ngx_str_t                           *override_charset;

  size_t                              content_type_len;
  ngx_str_t                           content_type;
```

```
    ngx_str_t                          charset;
    u_char                             *content_type_lowcase;
    ngx_uint_t                         content_type_hash;

    ngx_array_t                        cache_control;

    off_t                              content_length_n;
    time_t                             date_time;
    time_t                             last_modified_time;
} ngx_http_headers_out_t;
```

The next important step in our module is allocating memory for the response buffer. This memory should be allocated using Nginx's own APIs as mentioned in earlier chapters (since it also automatically takes care of freeing it). This can be done because the memory is allocated from a local memory pool, so that all memory allocations are tracked.

The response is created in a linked list or *chain* of buffers, each of which is of the size of ngx_buf_s. This allows Nginx to process the response in a parallel way. If there are other handlers or filters that need to postprocess the response, they can start their work as soon as the first buffer in the chain is ready, while you are filling up the second buffer. This allows Nginx to keep operating in a parallel fashion without waiting for any module to completely finish processing first.

When you are finished with creating the response in the last buffer, you should set b->last_buf = 1. This, as it is obvious from the name, will tell Nginx that this is the last response buffer from your module.

If the response processing was successful, you would want to set the status of the response header to HTTP_OK. This is done by r->headers_out.status = NGX_HTTP_OK.

You will then need to initiate the chain of header filters by calling ngx_http_send_header. This will indicate to Nginx that processing of the output headers has finished, and now Nginx can pass them to a chain of filters, which might want to do further postprocessing to the headers.

The final step is returning from the function by calling ngx_http_output_filter. This will initiate the process of the HTTP body filter chain. That is, Nginx or custom filter modules that might have been installed to do postprocessing on the HTTP response body you have just created in the buffer.

The summary of creating the Nginx custom module can be as follows:

1. Create a module configuration that is structured either for location , main, or server; each with a specific naming convention (see `ngx_http_hello_loc_conf_t`).

   The allowed directives of the module are in a static array of type `ngx_command_t` (see `ngx_http_hello_commands`). This will also have the function's pointers that will have the code to validate the value of each directive as well as initialize the handler.

2. Create a module context struct such as `ngx_http_<module name>_module_ctx` of type `ngx_http_module_t` which has a bunch of hooks for setting up configuration. Here you can have the post configuration hook, for example, to set up the main handler of your module (see `ngx_http_hello_module_ctx`).

3. Then we do the module definition, which is also a struct of type `ngx_module_t` and contains references to the module context and module commands that you created in the previous steps (see `ngx_http_hello_module`).

4. Create the main module handler function that processes the HTTP request. This function also outputs the response headers and body in a series of fixed size buffers.

Nginx Development Toolkit (NDK)

NDK is an Nginx module that makes it easier for the module developers to develop Nginx modules. As you have seen in this chapter so far, there are certain generic tasks that are repetitive as you are developing modules. NDK provides you with some built-in macros and functions that will reduce the amount of code you will have to write to develop a module.

In order to use NDK, you will have to add it as a module just like any other module. If you wish to use the macros and functions provided by this module, you will have to include the `ndk.h` file in your module source as well.

NDK provides useful utilities such as `conf` set functions for complex types such as paths and regular expressions, utility methods for NULL checking, returning values, and setting data to zero.

NDK also includes an **Auto Lib Core** that allows the developers and users to include external libraries in Nginx in a consistent, cross-platform manner.

You can see more details and documentation at `https://github.com/simpl/ngx_devel_kit`.

Summary

In this chapter we have learned the process of creating a simple Nginx handler module. We also looked at which basic structures a new module should define, and how to link them to each other. Finally, we looked at a small handler function that does a basic task, but provides you the basis of writing a much more complicated module.

If you are an Nginx module developer, you must extensively browse other modules and Nginx source code, which will help you learn how to do different things within your code and which API to use in general.

You will also find Nginx Development Kit at `https://github.com/simpl/ ngx_devel_kit`. This will provide you additional `conf_set` functions for regexes, complex/script values, paths, and macros to simplify tasks such as checking for NULL values when doing `ngx_array_push` and much more, which will simplify your life while writing custom Nginx modules.

Index

N

NDK
about 83, 104
Auto Lib Core 105
Nginx
about 83
Events module 19
installing, on Gentoo 13
installing, on MacOSX 13
Main module 15
modules, delegating 83
nginx.conf file 14
Nginx custom module
creating 104
Nginx Development Toolkit. *See* **NDK**
Nginx library
dependencies 9
nginx_lua module
directives 71-75
rewrite_by_lua_file directive 73
upstream Nginx modules, using 70
nginx_lua module, directives
access_by_lua 75
access_by_lua directive 74
content_by_lua 72
lua_package_path 71
rewrite_by_lua directive 73
set_by_lua 71, 72
Nginx module, components
configuration structures 90
directives 91-93
handler function 100-103
module context 94
module definition 98-100
Nginx modules
about 83, 84
filters 84
handlers 84
load balancers 84
Nginx PPA 7
Nginx request-handling phases
access 69
content 69
location rewrite 69
location selection 69
log 69

post action 69
post read 69
pre-access 69
server rewrite 69
server selection 69
try files 69
nginx -V command 14
Nginx yum repository
adding, for CentOS 6
adding, for RHEL 6
official Debian/Ubuntu packages 6
ngx_conf_log_error function 98
ngx_conf_set_flag_slot function 93
ngx_conf_set_num_slot function 93
ngx_conf_set_size_slot function 93
ngx_conf_set_str_slot function 93
ngx_http_auth_digest module
about 64
directives 64, 65
ngx_http_auth_digest module, directives
auth_digest 65
auth_digest_expires 65
auth_digest_replays 65
auth_digest_timeout 65
auth_digest_user_file 65
ngx_http_geoip_module
directives 76-80
using, for reverse IP lookup 76, 79
using, for reverse IP lookup 77-80
ngx_http_healthcheck_module 78, 79
**ngx_http_upstream_consistent_hash
module 81**
ngx_lua module
features 68
Nginx request-handling phases 69
ngx_pagespeed module
Beacon handler, configuring 67
console handler, configuring 67
handlers, configuring 67, 68
message handler, configuring 67
optimizations 66
speeding up 66
statics handler, configuring 67
ngx_postgres module
about 58
directives 58-60

Thank you for buying
Nginx Module Extension

About Packt Publishing

Packt, pronounced 'packed', published its first book *"Mastering phpMyAdmin for Effective MySQL Management"* in April 2004 and subsequently continued to specialize in publishing highly focused books on specific technologies and solutions.

Our books and publications share the experiences of your fellow IT professionals in adapting and customizing today's systems, applications, and frameworks. Our solution based books give you the knowledge and power to customize the software and technologies you're using to get the job done. Packt books are more specific and less general than the IT books you have seen in the past. Our unique business model allows us to bring you more focused information, giving you more of what you need to know, and less of what you don't.

Packt is a modern, yet unique publishing company, which focuses on producing quality, cutting-edge books for communities of developers, administrators, and newbies alike. For more information, please visit our website: www.packtpub.com.

About Packt Open Source

In 2010, Packt launched two new brands, Packt Open Source and Packt Enterprise, in order to continue its focus on specialization. This book is part of the Packt Open Source brand, home to books published on software built around Open Source licences, and offering information to anybody from advanced developers to budding web designers. The Open Source brand also runs Packt's Open Source Royalty Scheme, by which Packt gives a royalty to each Open Source project about whose software a book is sold.

Writing for Packt

We welcome all inquiries from people who are interested in authoring. Book proposals should be sent to author@packtpub.com. If your book idea is still at an early stage and you would like to discuss it first before writing a formal book proposal, contact us; one of our commissioning editors will get in touch with you.

We're not just looking for published authors; if you have strong technical skills but no writing experience, our experienced editors can help you develop a writing career, or simply get some additional reward for your expertise.

Instant Nginx Starter

ISBN: 978-1-78216-512-5   Paperback: 48 pages

Implement the nifty features of nginx with this focused guide

1. Learn something new in an Instant! A short, fast, focused guide delivering immediate results

2. Understand Nginx and its relevance to the modern web

3. Install Nginx and explore the different methods of installation

4. Configure and customize Nginx

Nginx HTTP Server
Second Edition

ISBN: 978-1-78216-232-2   Paperback: 318 pages

Make the most of your infrastructure and serve pages faster than ever with Nginx

1. Complete configuration directive and module reference

2. Discover possible interactions between Nginx and Apache to get the best of both worlds

3. Learn to configure your servers and virtual hosts efficiently

4. A step-by-step guide to switching from Apache to Nginx

Please check **www.PacktPub.com** for information on our titles

Printed in Great Britain
by Amazon.co.uk, Ltd.,
Marston Gate.